DAVID B. EAKIN and ROBERT LANGENFELD

George Moore's Correspondence with the Mysterious Countess

EDITIONS

ELS Editions
Department of English
University of Victoria
Victoria, BC
Canada V8W 3W1
www.elseditions.com

Founding Editor: Samuel L. Macey

General Editor: Luke Carson

Printed by CreateSpace

English literary studies monograph series
ISSN 0829-7681 ; 33
ISBN-10 0-920604-19-6
ISBN-13 978-0-920604-19-9

We dedicate
George Moore's Correspondence with the Mysterious Countess
to our mentor,
Helmut E. Gerber,
who originated the idea for this project several years ago.

CONTENTS

Acknowledgements   7

Introduction   9

Notes to Introduction   17

Textual Note   18

Letters   19

ACKNOWLEDGEMENTS

We are grateful to the Humanities Research Center, The University of Texas at Austin, for permission to publish Gabrielle's letters, and to Ms. Cathy Henderson, Research Associate at the Center, in particular for her assistance in securing the letters. We are also grateful to the late J. C. Medley, George Moore's literary executor, and to the National Library of Ireland, especially Alf Mac Lochlainn (Director) and D. O. Launaigh (Keeper), for permission to publish Moore's letters.

A very special thanks goes to the always helpful authority on George Moore, Edwin Gilcher. His *A Bibliography of George Moore* (De Kalb: Northern Illinois University Press, 1970) is an invaluable aid to all Moore scholars. Moreover, he generously agreed to read our manuscript and made many useful suggestions that improved our work.

INTRODUCTION

George Moore's relationship with Lady Cunard is well known and well remembered. There are, of course, other women in Moore's life, relationships of varying similarities and marked differences, that are not well known to Moore scholars. In Joseph Hone's *The Life of George Moore* some attention is given to Virginia Crawford.[1] She avidly worked for political and charitable concerns, on occasion was a translator, published in reputable periodicals like the *Pall Mall Gazette*, *Fortnightly Review*, and *Dublin Review*, and was Moore's paid researcher and invaluable secretary for forty years.[2] Three relationships of a very distinctive kind, unlike Moore's lifelong passion for Lady Cunard or his businesslike friendship with Virginia Crawford, are also important to Moore scholarship. In his forthcoming *George Moore on Parnassus*, Professor Helmut E. Gerber presents Moore's correspondence with two women of special interest, Hildegarde Hawthorne and Emily Lorenz Meyer.

Moore's relationship with the granddaughter of Nathaniel Hawthorne, begun in 1907, is almost totally epistolary. They met once during the summer of 1913 in Paris, but the rendezvous was a disappointment for both. Although Moore does write of his literary projects and offers her advice on her own journalistic and literary work, by and large the letters are sensuous and suggestive, often picturing a man in his late fifties attempting to rekindle a spirit of youth. He repeatedly comments on her shapely legs and athletic body as insufficiently revealed in photographs she has sent him. Their correspondence is something of an "epistolary affair," each romanticizing the other, each almost fictionalizing the other. For Moore, their exchanges appear to be an epistolary game.

This gamesmanship is also evident in Moore's correspondence with Emily Lorenz Meyer, a Bostonian married to a German, who initiated the exchange as the admirer of a famous author about the same time as Hawthorne. Again he receives a photograph; a familiarity emerges between the two; he tries to become what he terms her "father confessor"; he elicits personal information on her marital status and details of a love intrigue; he asks her to translate *Elizabeth Cooper* into German (which she did not); and he imagines circumstances under which they might meet (which they did not). The language of this correspondence, however, is less sensuous. Still, the curious mixture of personal and literary relationships with Meyer is analogous to that with Hawthorne.

The third and most mysterious epistolary relationship was chronologically first. The initial correspondent was an Austrian countess, the exact identity of whom is still undetermined. Moore addressed her, to begin with, as "Chère Baronne," and subsequently as "My dear Baronne" and "My dear Gabrielle." While the typed copies of the letter to Moore, located in the Humanities Research Center of the University of Texas at Austin,[3] are labeled "Gabrielle, Countess von Hoenstadt," other sources suggest this was not her actual name. A 1936 letter from Mona Jackson, Moore's former secretary, to Hone refers to Moore's correspondence with a "Gabrielle Vassal."[4] More recently, a Sotheby sale in London on 19 and 20 May 1977 turned up presentation copies of *The Untilled Field, The Lake,* and *Elizabeth Cooper,* with the following respective inscriptions: "To the Baronne Franzi Ripp with George Moores kind regards November 1903"; "To 'Gabrielle' (La Baronne Franzi Ripp) with George Moore's kind regards. Jan. 1st 1905"; "To Gabrielle Her Comedy from George Moore July 1913." Adding confusion is one of her letters to Moore, dated 26 December [1903], where she signs her name "Cécile" and indicates that "Gabrielle" is her second name. This puzzling array of names makes it virtually impossible to determine her true name in full. No biographical information on her has been located.[5] From internal evidence, though, we learn much about this unidentified admirer of Moore.

Even though the lady in question cannot be identified, the correspondence does merit study. The letters are valuable to Moore scholarship for three basic reasons. First, they adumbrate similar strategies Moore would later use with Hawthorne and Meyer, thus embellishing our ever-growing knowledge of his epistolary relationships. Second, Moore used many portions of her letters to create the dialogue for *The Coming of Gabrielle,* often quoting her letters verbatim. Finally, Moore himself planned to publish the letters.

Only twelve letters by Moore to Gabrielle have been discovered thus far, all in the National Library of Ireland.[6] (Several incomplete and inaccurate transcriptions of them have been published in Hone's *The Life of George Moore.*) The twelve letters cover two and one half years, from late 1903 to early 1906. It seems likely, though not certain, that the correspondence lasted much longer, since Mona Jackson refers to Moore's receiving letters from "Gabrielle Vassal" "a year or two before he died."[7] Nevertheless, in the letters available several tactics on Moore's part emerge which foreshadow strategies he would later use when writing to Hawthorne and Meyer.

Initially he tries to persuade Gabrielle that they are "kindred spirits," saying, "I need not tell you that I have never met you in the flesh but your spirit I have known always — you are, to put it bluntly, one of my women." In this first letter, Moore goes on to say that being a divorcée with no children "poetises" her, that they have before them an untapped source for personal communion. It is with this same sentiment that he repeatedly asks for her photograph, in the first and subsequent letters. When he does receive the picture, he is delighted: "the photograph is deliciously like you; I can see that though I've never seen you." His interest in photographs is partly prurient, partly a means to extrapolate the psychological from the physical. Later, with Hawthorne and Meyer, he would become more adept in using the solicited photograph to further the intimacy of shared confidences.

Also first evident in these letters are suggestions of a possible meeting. In one letter he fantasizes about an imaginary meeting in London, but generally he encouraged her to think any meeting would be disillusioning. If only she had been born a little earlier or he a little later: "I might have inspired those desires which I think you would like me to inspire and without which I am afraid my presence would be but an embarrassment." Moore was genuinely concerned that he was getting old and romantically unattractive. Still, there is evidence that he was occupied not so much with her possible disillusionment but with the possible termination of their epistolary love affair, the waning of passion in her letters. He did not want to be looked upon as just a kindly old man of letters, nor did he want to lose psychological insight that might arise from more intimate correspondence.

Moore obviously took pleasure in writing his letters to her, for they are generally long and well written, based mainly on "literature and personality." He delights in quoting sensuous passages from Swinburne, suggesting she recite them in bed at night. He assures her that only by confiding in him can her personality be properly expressed. The frank woman is most charming: "You need have no fear anyone will see your letters so write the thoughts that pass through your mind however 'naughty' they may be," writes Moore, "and I hope they will be very naughty."

Perhaps most importantly he was interested in soliciting the confidence of Gabrielle in an effort to explore the feminine psyche. She inspired his romantic comedy *Elizabeth Cooper* (published in 1913 but an earlier version was set in type in 1904). The play was reworked and retitled *The Coming of Gabrielle* (1920). It is the story of a Viennese woman who writes to a famous English author and arranges a rendezvous. The hesitant author instead sends his younger male secretary, who poses as the author, proposes to the woman, and, after complications and revealed identities, eventually marries her. Moore worked out in literature what he could not, or would not, in reality. Mona Jackson, in her important letter to Hone, confirms that much of the dialogue was taken directly from Gabrielle's letters. Indeed, he initially considered making a short story out of them but finally abandoned that idea for another: to publish her letters with an introduction.

On reflection, Moore's relationship with Gabrielle seems to have been one of father-confessor, a role which afforded him personal as well as literary satisfaction. The same role is even more obvious in his letters to Hawthorne and Meyer. In a passage of her letter to Hone marked *"Private,"* Jackson offers a telling comment on how Moore viewed his epistolary relationship:

> I do remember that whilst I was working for him a year or two before he died, he often used to receive letters signed "Gabrielle Vassal," and seemed rather impatient and annoyed when he saw her handwriting — as if he had got all he wanted from a literary point of view, from her correspondence, and could not be bothered further.[8]

It would not be outrageous to conclude Gabrielle's letters interested George Moore literarily, perhaps more so than they interested him personally.

When Gabrielle first writes to Moore, she is probably twenty-eight years of age (born 26 September 1875), tall, "a meter 77," she notes, has reddish hair, and claims she is "not a beauty": "I am very white and rosy but I have freckles and my eyes are small and sly and *myopes*." Those sly eyes have "tiny wrinkles" about them, because she has "so much aplomb now and experiences." She says she has the face of a cat, while, after seeing a photograph of Moore, he has the face of a horse.

Her family was French, "but my ancestors did emigrate 1600 and something (it was for a particular reason but I realy have forgotten

what it was) and settled in Bohemia, where they got a beautiful place."
She speaks rarely of her father but refers often to brother Niki and a
cousin, Marietta. Her mother, "grand to look at," visits her in Vienna,
though their relationship is strained because Gabrielle has recently
divorced her husband, "Count H."

Through Gabrielle's faltering English emerges a woman who is coy,
teasing with a wise innocence; playful, like a young girl; serious, possess-
ing a need to convert men for what she interprets as the better; motherly,
seemingly compelled to dream of another marriage with children; tem-
pestuous, admitting to a bad temper, and at times tearfully immersed in
ennui. Divorce, marriage, and children are main topics of her letters,
though she does read and discuss some of Moore's works. It is obvious
the divorce was not well received, although she and her husband parted
by "*commun accord*." Yet Gabrielle seems to be obsessed with marriage,
at one point saying, "I should invent marriage if it had not been invented
long ago." Ironically, while asserting she was "dreadfully in love" with
her husband and "so wanted him to marry to save us both," not long
afterward she fell in love anew, with one "H.H." She coquettishly con-
tinues: "(it was not a practical arrangement — do you think so?) I
loved him [H.H.] dearly but I simply didn't know at that time that a
married lady can have a lover. He made rather tame love to me."

Two years later Gabrielle and her husband moved to Prague, and
there she fell "violently in love" with "Darling F." She knew and liked
his wife and three children. (Mrs. "F." was also expecting another
child.) "Darling F.," however, turned out to be a "liar and rogue."
Before he and his family moved to Brasilien, he magnanimously had his
son write and deliver a farewell letter. Their parting, she says, was her
"first great sorrow." At the time she is writing to Moore, she has a new
"friend," as she terms him, a "sly dear old boy," who repeatedly admon-
ished her not to write to Moore, for he could not be tenderhearted: "the
English never are."

It seems clear we do not have Gabrielle's first letter to Moore. In the
first four letters we do have, she writes about *Esther Waters, Evelyn
Innes* (a novel she has a special affinity for), *The Untilled Field*, and
Confessions of a Young Man. Generally, though, her letters do not con-
cern themselves with Moore's literature; they dwell on more intimate
matters. On a personal level, Gabrielle is ambivalent toward Moore, if
not contradictory. In the letter of 11 December [1903], she is forward:
"But I think I know what I want: to sit with you in a dark room and

kiss you fervently." A few sentences later, however, she reveals a passion for Moore the author, saying, "it would be a catastrophe if I were to fall in love with the *man* in you. I will only be in love with the author."

Gabrielle capriciously alters moods, at times being coy, occasionally miffed that Moore does not answer her letters, at other times hinting at her willingness to marry him, to hear his confessions and pamper him. "You must think of me," she writes, "and not only of your books. You must be fond of me, as fond if not fonder as of your heroines. Are you a little fond of me Mr. Moore? Would you like to sit near me, to hold my hand and to tell me all of your troubles? Tell me please." Again, though, she is not constant in the mother-confessor role. She writes the letter of 25 January [1904] with Moore's photograph before her and ends it by saying, "A dreadful thing happened a moment ago. I kissed your photograph!"

Her coquettish suggestions later became flirtations with marriage. In her 14 January [1904] letter, after alluding to the fact that she has revealed their correspondence to her cousin and cousin's friend, Gabrielle seems to propose marriage, though to be sure in a circumspect fashion: "But they don't know of course that I asked you to come to Vienna (this *espacially* they must not know,) and that we want to marry or not to marry — which is it? I don't remember. I am dreadfully *en l'air ces jours ci.*" Her next letter, eleven days later, does not mention marriage. Instead, Gabrielle admonishes Moore not to write "from morning till night." She counsels and orders further: "Really I must scold you a little. I don't want you to fall ill. You may write 4 or 5 hours every day but no more. One must walk every day for 2 hours at least."

A few weeks afterward, Gabrielle begins to apologize for writing to Moore too frequently: "I hope you won't swear at my writing too often now!" By 10 February [1904] she becomes churlish, accusing Moore of waning interest, and ends the letter abruptly: " — you don't like me. Good-bye, dear Mr. Moore." Her doubts are expressed more thoughtfully in the next letter:

> I am not ashamed to run after you, but I very soon will be ashamed of thinking so much of a man without even knowing if he deserves it. It makes me feel what I don't want to be: *a little fool.*

In early March, however, her mood is again peevish:

> I hate disgusting things and I think I told you so a long time ago. Please mind it for the future. Good-bye. I am a little stupid sometimes but I like

me to be like that. I have been crying, my nose is swollen and I have hardly any eyes. I am like ladies of Dublin to-day — not desirable! I will not write a nice letter to-day.

Her letters and her moods continue to vacillate — indeed through the last known letter to Moore.

Moore and Gabrielle never met. They discussed meeting in Paris and in Vienna. On one occasion, Gabrielle offers other possible places for rendezvous: Munich, Regensburg, Nuremberg. It seems certain he never meant to meet the mysterious Gabrielle, the lady whose identity he intended to remain a mystery. He had her letters typed, and most likely the originals will never be discovered. That is how Moore wished it to be. Still, he valued her correspondence for its psychological revelations. Perhaps, too, in the last years of his life he looked on Gabrielle's letters with an old man's sentimentality. At the conclusion of her typed correspondence appears Moore's final word on Gabrielle:

And at the end of all this correspondence came a little note of thanks for my sending of *The Lake*. She understood *The Lake* to be a parable: that every man has in his heart a lake that he cannot or can cross, and all his life afterwards depends upon his crossing or turning aside. I missed a great deal certainly. If I appealed to the wisdom of Yeats (the wisest man in Ireland,) he would say: We must yield a little to gain a great deal. But what have I gained? All those books, twenty or twenty-five volumes — it doesn't matter which. It is what I would have got in return that matters: an armful of warm love, and Gabrielle would have been that thirty years ago. Now she is sixty, and has forgotten me and forgotten love. Or maybe she is dead, and her death would be the worst thing that could happen to me, for out of the golden bar of heaven she would watch for me and be interested still in her letters. Will he keep or will he destroy them? she would ask, and were I to throw all this bundle into yon fire she would shriek and run from the gold bar of heaven and become a wraith or a ghost that would torment me, that would seek night and day to revenge herself. I would dream of Gabrielle always, and on awakening would fall back into sleep to redeem my dreams of her. It would be intolerable! I must please her at all costs, and the only end she would see in vanity, and in mine, would be publication. The letters shall go to the printer to-morrow.

NOTES TO THE INTRODUCTION

[1] Joseph Hone, *The Life of George Moore* (New York: Macmillan, 1936), pp. 353-54, 356-59, *et passim*.

[2] Further information on Crawford, Hawthorne, and Meyer can be found in Helmut E. Gerber's *George Moore on Parnassus*, which will be published by Associated University Presses and is now in the pageproof stage. We worked with the late Professor Gerber on this important work, but the Gabrielle letters were not available at that time.

[3] We are grateful to the Humanities Research Center, The University of Texas at Austin, for permission to publish Gabrielle's letters, and to Ms. Cathy Henderson, Research Associate at the Center, in particular for her assistance in securing the letters.

[4] Letter to Joseph Hone, 14 February 1935, University of Washington, Seattle.

[5] Professor Helmut E. Gerber attempted to discover Gabrielle's identity, but even the diligent assistance of Professor Werner Bies (Universität Trier) was to no avail. *Ruvigny's Titled Nobility of Europe, Burke's Peerage & Baronetage* (105th ed.), and *Debrett's Peerage & Baronetage* offered no clue to Gabrielle's true identity. In a letter to Langenfeld, Edwin Gilcher, the authoritative bibliographer of Moore (*A Bibliography of George Moore*, NIU Press, 1970), reflected on the confusion inherent in this matter: " 'Countess von Hoenstadt' is obviously the name created for her by GM for his literary purpose. It seems as though the name inscribed on the presentation copies, 'Baronne Franzi Ripp,' was her actual name in 1903 and still her name in 1913. If the Gabrielle Vassal of the later letters is the same person, she could have married in the meantime. Or it may have just been a coincidence of two women having the same name, a possibility that should be considered." Old public records in Vienna might reveal Gabrielle's identity, but they were not available to us.

[6] We are grateful to the National Library of Ireland for permission to publish Moore's letters, and Alf Mac Lochlainn (Director) and D. O. Launaigh (Keeper) in particular. We are as well indebted to the late J. C. Medley, Moore's literary executor, for permision to publish the letters.

[7] Letter to Joseph Hone, 14 February 1935, University of Washington, Seattle.

[8] Letter to Joseph Hone, 14 February 1935, University of Washington, Seattle.

Textual Note: There are thirty-four letters altogether, twelve by Moore and twenty-two by Gabrielle. We have ordered the letters chronologically in the sequence they were received. We have also printed the letters *ipsissima verba*, except for a few silent corrections of Moore's inadvertent misspellings. Gabrielle's misspellings we have left intact since they are preserved in the typescript made under Moore's direction. We have also followed the typescript in italicizing the numerous foreign words and expressions in Gabrielle's macaronic prose style. We have standardized all headings, dates, and titles in both Moore's and Gabrielle's letters. All dots are the letter-writer's; information supplied by us within any letter is bracketed. The original twelve Moore letters are all Autograph Letters Signed.

Letter 1

Gabrielle to Moore   [mid-November 1903]

Dear Mr. Moore,

I am so glad you have written! You realy are very kind and I thank you very much. I am rather proud to have a *lettre* from you now but I am a little (not too much) perplexed, for I see now *you are not a priest*. There was a time I almost imagined you as a priest, not a monk of course but something *aufwärts* of Monsignor. But you are staying in Paris, staying at an hotel. So I must have been mistaken.

I have been thinking of you a good deal since I wrote that first letter and I now read *Esther Waters*.[1] I like it. But I have a new idea (I hope you will find it a capital one) about Evelyn Innes.[2] I don't want her any more to leave the convent. It would spoil the story if she did. But she could write her diary! or rather a sort of memoires. I am afraid it is *not* a thing a nun is allowed to do, but so many people will not know and you and I we need not tell. You see, in sleepless nights to escape evil thoughts, etc, she jumps out of her bed (is not my English elegant?) and she scribbles pages and pages (I should *like* two volumes but four I should *love*.) Of course she must tell us plenty about her *past* life, espacially very exciting things about the two years in Paris you have *übersprungen* to my greatest sorrow. The new book, you know, you could *widmen* to me. Could you not now? You see, as a well trained if not very fervent Roman Catholic I should prefer all nuns to be angels and the women without a talent for angels to be wives. But now you did make her a nun you can leave her in the convent. Only please let her dye in

---

[1] First published in March 1894, with subsequent, revised editions in May 1899 and June 1920, *Esther Waters* (which Moore considered naming "Mother and Child") is the naturalistic story of a servant raising her illegitimate child and contending with social inequities.

[2] Gabrielle apparently initiated her correspondence with Moore after reading the Tauchnitz edition of *Evelyn Innes* (Leipzig, 1898).

five years, *au plus*. You don't know perhaps but I do. At thirty-five she will get *hysterisch* (poor soul) — a thing which in German means something much more dreadful than it does in English. You forgot to tell me if you like German and so I must *plagen* myself again, which I don't like very much. But do you know, Mr. Moore, I have suddenly rather changed my opinions about you. I don't believe any longer that you are above all a very religious man. You simply may be wonderfully *vielseitig* and interested in all sorts of things, in religions, love and music, in prima donnas, race horses and poor hardworking servants. I should like to be like you.

Your question whether I sometimes come to Paris made me laugh aloud! It seemed so refreshing. Could I go to Paris? Well, Mr. Moore, I am afraid I could not. You see, it's not yet a year since I was obliged to divorce, and my family has not yet overcome the shock, and I have to be very careful indeed for two years or three at least. They are all looking at me, wondering what I shall be doing next! Going to Paris would not be the right thing. But come you to Vienna? Will you? I am sure you have some friends here. You have me at all events, and a cousin of mine who admires you very much and often speaks for hours about *Evelyn Innes*. I think it is rather meddling and very impertinent since it is *my* book.

In the "Following of Christ" there is quite an amusing passage. It seems to be for men so do listen please. "Be not interested in one woman particularly, but recommend all good women in general to God."[3] Well, most men *do not* and I am glad of it. I should not like to be interesting merely because I am a good woman and to be cared for in general just as if I was sheep. I have friends of course and they often come to see me. So you could come too. I hope you are past 40? I don't like very young men, it is not my *faute*. You may be horrid. But I will see directly if you are. I am not a baby. *A propos* of baby (I very nearly forgot) — it certainly is a pity that Evelyn didn't get any. But I won't scold you — it is too late now, and Sir Owen[4] perhaps did not ask for your advice. Did he? I wonder! Yes, I see it is too late now, but she could dream she has

---

[3] Gabrielle may be referring to a translation of *Imitatio Christi*, by St. Bernard de Clairvaus (1091-1153). We have been unable to locate the translation which she quotes from.

[4] Owen Asher is the name of Evelyn's seducer in *Evelyn Innes* and was modeled on Sir William Eden, a dilettante and social figure whom Moore knew as early as the 1890's.

a child. And then, you know, she must be jealous. Every woman sometimes is. I so often wondered how Evelyn would behave, being dreadfully
jealous. She might be jealous now in the convent thinking of her lovers
consoling themselves, etc. If you come to Vienna we shall speak so much
about Evelyn. But not in English I hope? I never, *au grand jamais,*
speak a word of English! Please come. Vienna is interesting and the
Opera is famous, as you surely know. But I am not a rich lady living in
a house of her own and all sort of things. I live alone just by myself. I
never had children though I have been married for nearly six years.
Somehow the *liebe Gott* (he is so much less formidable than your "God"
tout court) failed to see how much I was in need of some. And now it's
all over for me. I have a dog. Mrs. Delicia has Spartan but *your* heroines
are not fond of dogs. Please write to me once more. To-day I give my
full address, but on an extra sheet of paper to prove how very prudent a
young lady I am! I hope I have not bored you? This is a long letter and
you don't like *longueurs*!

Good-bye, dear Mr. Moore, and please don't turn out to be a lady
suddenly. Could you do such a thing? It would spoil me everything.

Yours sincerely

Gabrielle von Hoenstadt

It is the first time in my life that I write to a *auteur*. Once I wished to
write to Tolstoi but afterwards I forgot about it.

Letter 2

Moore to Gabrielle   Saturday [late November 1903]
                                      Hotel Continental, Paris

Chère Baronne,

I received your interesting letter a few days ago and if it had not been
for some difficult writing which kept me at work till the end of the day
and left me weary and distracted I should have answered you sooner.
Your letter is still a pleasure. I look into it, turn it over and think about
it, for it reveals a woman I know. I need not tell you that I have never
met you in the flesh but your spirit I have known always — you are, to
put it somewhat bluntly, one of my women and you recognized yourself
as one, if you had not you would not have written to me. Our lives are

little sympathetic circles and into these circles kindred spirits pass and sometimes remain for a little while. You already know me — you have guessed that I am not religious — that I am one who is interested in those whose lives lie outside of his life — poor working folk, nuns and peasants trying to scrape a living out of a soil — you do not speak of *The Untilled Field*.[1] I will send it to you on Monday. It is about Ireland in whose frail body the religious spirit burns intensely, wearing it away as might a mortal malady. I am half minded to send you a book I wrote some years ago *Confession[s] d'un Jeune Anglais*.[2] The English edition is out of print but the French translation is very good. The book exists but the *jeune anglais* has disappeared. On second thoughts I will not send it. You need not know everything about me; a little mystery does no one any harm. That you divorced your husband or was divorced by him surrounds you with attractions to which I am still susceptible, and that you have not had children poetises you in my eyes; and I shall brood on my fair correspondent [indecipherable] to Ireland. I went there three years ago;[3] my exile was occasioned by the Boer war;[4] finding myself thinking differently from my friends and the mass of Englishmen I went away. Whether I shall continue to live there or come to Paris, where my youth was spent I know not. But I must return to Ireland next week to finish a tale entitled *The Lake*[5] — a tale you will like I think. Sometimes I go to Germany to hear music — I have been to Bayreuth many times and to Munich.[6] But I don't know German and to live in a country and

---

[1] First published 20 April 1903 by T. Fisher Unwin, *The Untilled Field* was once called by Moore "not a collection of short stories" but "a book about Ireland in the form of short stories." Moore believed it showed "the influence of priestly rule in an objective form." Among the stories that deal with the clergy are "In the Clay," "Some Parishioners," "A Letter to Rome," "Julia Cahill's Curse," and "A Play-House in the Waste."

[2] *Confessions of a Young Man* was first published in book form in 1888 by Swan Sonnenschein. This early autobiography chronicles his seven-year sojourn in Paris from 1873 to 1880 and his return to London. The French translation was first published in 1889.

[3] Between 1899 and 1901 Moore made frequent trips to Dublin in his effort to help found the Irish Literary Theatre with Yeats, Lady Gregory, and Edward Martyn. He did not set up residence at 4 Upper Ely Place, Dublin, until the spring of 1901.

[4] For detailed information on Moore's hostility to the English involvement in the Boer War, see Joseph O. Baylen, "George Moore, W. T. Stead, and the Boer War," *Studies in English*, 3 (1962), 49-60.

[5] First published on 10 November 1905 by William Heinemann. Originally intended as one of the stories in *The Untilled Field*, *The Lake* is the tale of an Irish Catholic priest and his psychological struggle with his religious doubts.

not speak the language is trying to one whose greatest pleasure is conversation. I can tell by your letter that you are a conversationalist and if we were to meet we should find much to say. You would know, as you say you would, if I were horrid and at once. But my dear Baronne I am not horrid; I used to fear I was when I was very young but since then I have found out that I am not. But it wouldn't be sufficient to find out at the end of a long journey into an unknown country that you did not think me horrid would it? Moreover I dare not undertake the journey you propose — what a fatuous journey it would be! Imagine me presenting myself and watching your face not daring to ask you if you were disappointed. I am not fatuous nor courageous enough. You express a hope that I shall not turn out to be a woman "and spoil everything." There is no danger of that — my sex is above suspicion. One of these days you will come to Paris, you will let me know, and in this hope I propose to live for the present. I return to Ireland next week and I hope you will write to me. To close this long letter I will make a request — will you send me your photograph. I will send you my book on Monday if you in return send me your photograph. A photograph gives an imperfect idea of the reality, for a photograph does not speak, and no one knows what she is like till she has spoken.[7]

Very sincerely yours,

George Moore

[6] Moore often attended the Wagner festivals with his cousin Edward Martyn, Lady Cunard's party, or Lord Howard de Walden.

[7] Brief excerpts of this letter are inaccurately transcribed in Hone's *Life*, p. 246.

Letter 3

Gabrielle to Moore   [early December 1903]
                                        Vienna

Dear Mr. Moore,
    You are very cruel. You tease me very much. Why do you mention *Confessions d'un Jeune Anglais* if you do not send the book? I want to read it but they do not have it here. I asked at different booksellers and I shall be obliged to wait very long till it comes from Paris. I hate waiting. The other book has not yet arrived. But your *lettre*, Mr. Moore, is

charming. It's just the *lettre* I expected. Thank you a 1000 times for saying that I am one of your women. I am of course, and besides I am in love with you. Don't you think so too? My first idea after reading your letter was to send you a *télégramme* or to rush to the next telefon to beg of you to come in spite of all. But it would have been so aggressiv if I had done and so I tried to calm myself and succeeded after a while. But I had a sleepless night. Am I not rather ridiculous? Please, dear Mr. Moore, don't bother about my coming to Paris. I shall never do that. We must meet here and you will come in spring. Now it's always raining and Vienna is so dirty when it does. But in spring it is lovely and I know you will come, and what is more, feel at home here at once. You will like me very much of course because you could not dislike one of your own women. But I am very, very tall and if you are not it will irritate you. I only send a little bit of a foto to-day. It is not very good but you don't deserve a better one. You teased me about the book. *Osez donc dire* that you didn't! Another photograph (and a much bigger one) will be sent to you a week after I have finished to read *Les Confessions*, not a day sooner.

I congratulate you about your sex being above suspicion! Mine is not always I am afraid. I like so much to look at graceful ballet girls. Please don't despise me, but I prefer the ballet in *Robert der Teufel*[1] to Wagner's *Siegfried*. *Tristan and Isolde* I should like I guess. But I have never heard it. I have lived in lonely castles and in convents till I was eighteen and after my marriage I have been at small places mostly (*garnisons*, you know.) This year I travelled. I have been to Venice in May with my youngest brother and in Germany in summer. I ought to have written to you long before now. I am sure we should have met long ago if I had. But somehow I didn't dare. And when your first letter arrived my hands turned as cold as ice and my cheeks burning hot. Is it not a funny thing to have cold hands and a hot face at the same time? A moment later I made *gambades* and pinched my dog because I was so happy. But I can't stand a man with a large beard and if you have one, Mr. Moore, you had better say so at once. And tell me your age. *I* was borne on the twenty-sixth of September, 1875. You see, my age is quite respectable. Please, does fair mean pretty or blonde? I don't know, but I am both though I am not a beauty. I am very white and rosy but I have

---

[1] Giacomo Meyerbeer's long five-act opera, first performed in Paris (1831), and usually seen under the title *Robert de Diable*.

freckles and my eyes are small and sly and *myopes*. They are not like Evelyn's.

You tell me in your letter that you will brood on me when you have returned home. Are you in Dublin already? I hope you are. Please brood on me. Begin at once. I shall think of it and it will be like kisses. (I am so glad none of my aunts will see that letter. It's a rather naughty one. Do you think me naughty? The truth is I can be much more naughty still.) I have a very dear friend, Mr. Moore. He lives rather far away but he came to see me last week. I told him about you and he made such naughty nostrils (it *is* nostrils I mean.) It was so amusing, but of course if I can help it I shall not make him jealous *tout de bon*. He has left already and I feel sad to-day. Is Dublin a lovely place? Are you married, Mr. Moore? Write a lot of things about yourself, will you? And could you not send your foto too? Please do. It doesn't matter if you are not beautiful. My husband was and is but it made no difference whatever. *Nous avons divorcé d'un commun accord*, and I now wonder why we haven't done it sooner. Good-bye, dear Mr. Moore, I am sleepy. I so hope I shall sleep to-night. Will you brood on me when you awake in the night? I hope you don't work till late in the morning. I could not allow such a thing on account of your nerfs. (I am ashamed of my spelling but I can't help it.) Good-bye again and if the foto is a disappointment throw it into the fire. You will have another one in a fortnight or so. Do you know what a *blu'hendes Veib*[2] is? You ought to know if you have been to Bayreuth. I am one, and how much! But you will see in spring. Make me a promise, will you, that you will come to Vienna in the spring. I should like it so very much.

Sincerely yours

Gabrielle von Hoenstadt

[2] Meaning blossoming woman or wife.

Letter 4

Gabrielle to Moore   11 Decembre [1903]

Dear Mr. Moore,

I am so tired of the rain and I am tired of myself and of everything indeed except you.

Do come soon. I have had *des misères* this week. I couldn't write. . . .
But I think I know what I want: to sit with you in a dark room and kiss
you fervently. I have never seen your face, I don't know what your
figure is like, I have never heard your voice. I won't see and hear you. It
would be a catastrophe if I were to fall in love with the *man* in you. I
will only be in love with the author. You dear Mr. Moore, please live
very long and don't disappoint me, never. You must write a heap of
books. I like reading but I have no patience with other authors' books.
You are not like them, you are quite, quite different. I had such nice
little surprises in reading *The Untilled Field*. At first I didn't read it
properly, I merely selected some of the stories, "The Marriage Feast,"
"The Wedding Gown," and "The Wild Goose" because there is a baby
in it and some *musik*. But now I have read all and I like it so, so much.
"The Window" is very good. And what a darling of a husband your Ned
is! He takes his wife upon his knee — he comes into her bed! Other
authors' husbands are doing such sweet, natural little things. They are
either beasts or *poseurs* and hypocrites. O, I have no patience with them.
I wish I could throw something to their head. Do you know what you
could do, Mr. Moore? A thing no author yet has done quite to my
satisfaction: write a story about a married couple, but a long, beautiful,
might-be-true story. (I don't know if that is a real word? At all events
try not to be envious when I invent new words!) You see, I don't want
the husband to be a saint nor the wife to be an angel, I just want them
to be a man and a woman (I am not a bit perverse!) to quarrel as well
as to kiss, to have temptations both. But the end must be a *happy* end. I
don't want a *Kreutzer Sonata*[1] again. And they must not be peasants,
please. I should prefer not, and on some children I must insist. Don't
say, Mr. Moore, that you can't do it because you hate marriage. You
hate convents too and yet you have written *Sister Teresa*. And will you
publish a big volume — "*Lettres* of Owen Asher to Evelyn Innes," and
a nobler one, much bigger still, "Evelyn's *lettres* to her lovers (and
confesseurs)"? I should be quite happy if you would!

Do you know what I shall do now? I don't want to be a *faulpelz* when
you are so busy. I shall begin to take English lessons to-day and *leçons
de piano* next week. I like to play. Chopin, Grieg and Mendelsohn are
my favorites, but till now I used to say that I love them in a platonic

---

[1] Tolstoi's oldest son played Beethoven's *Kreutzer Sonata* and the author was deeply
impressed. The novelette (1899) is a dramatic account of the sufferings a man
endures because of his unfaithful wife, whom he eventually stabs.

way, which meant nothing at all but was intended to mean that I don't play them very well. I hope I shall make *des progrès*. And if you come, Mr. Moore, you will not stay in Grand Hotel, Hotel Bristol, Krantz, Imperial or Sacher. I shouldn't like to *caramboler* with my brothers and friends *en sortant de chez vous*. You will stay in Meissl and Schadn, neuer Markt, to please your little friend. I have a headache so I must say good-bye. I hope you are not angry with me. I hope the proposal has not made you *popfschen*. I am not a widow yet and probably I shall never be. Besides if we are too much of the same kin we couldn't marry (there is the doctrine of Schopenhauer's,[2] you know.) To-day *überhaupt* I don't think that I would care to be your wife. I am always changing my moods and opinions. It is amusing but a little *fatiguant* too. It is like changing one's dress a dozen times *par jour*. Good-bye now, dear Mr. Moore.

Yours truly

Gabrielle

[2] This may refer to Schopenhauer's belief that women unconsciously seek men who differ from them. The marriage of two people too much alike does not allow the woman to "neutralize his defects." See *The World as Will and Representation*, ed. E. F. J. Payne (New York: Dover, 1958), II, p. 544.

Letter 5

Moore to Gabrielle

Thursday [mid-December 1903]
12 Waterloo Place, S.W.
London

My dear Baronne,

I am writing to you from Sir Owen Asher's[1] rooms — his real name is not Asher, that goes without saying. He is at present in Dresden with his wife and children, and wishing to finish a piece of writing before I went back to Ireland I took the liberty to use his rooms during the day: writing in an hotel is not pleasant. I hope he won't think it a liberty; I don't think he will — I hope he will think it a compliment. His rooms are papered with a dainty French grey paper, a white muslin with bones

[1] See Letter 1, note 4.

laid on a dark ground and lovely little pictures face one: Corot,[2] Diaz,[3] Fantin-Latour[4] and water colours by Brabazon[5] whom we admire. The windows overlook Waterloo Place — the heart of London; one can see the trees of the Green Park; and there is something auspicious in the situation and the refinement of the rooms — they are a man's rooms but they are rooms that would please a woman, especially a woman like you. We could not meet in more harmonious surroundings. I can see you sitting by the fire; your legs are crossed and your skirt hangs prettily over your foot and the little sly eyes watch me and thoughtfully.

My dear Baronne we are the same kin, and your instinct led you aright; but you should have been born a little earlier in the century or I a little later. If we had found each other out twelve years ago[6] when I wrote *Confessions d'un Jeune Anglais* I might have inspired those desires which I think you would like me to inspire and without which I am afraid my presence would be but an embarrassment. Have you met a man who seemed to correspond to your idea of what a lover should be and who when he was not there you felt you could love but who did not draw you to him when he sat opposite you. Looking at him you have not been able to find a reason why you should not take him in your arms only you did not want to; and you have been puzzled by the remembrance of one who although he does not correspond to your idea nevertheless drew you irresistibly . . . That you would like me if we were to meet I do not doubt. We are clearly of the same kin, but I doubt very much if you would feel drawn to me and if you were not you would be disappointed. You want to know if I am tall and if I wear a beard. I am tall and I do not wear a beard. The absense of the beard I can prove by a photograph — no I can't the photograph was taken some years ago — I will send it to you when I get to Dublin, but it will not enlighten you

[2] Camille Corot (1796-1875), French painter known for his landscapes and his pre-Impressionistic techniques. See Moore's "Ingres and Corot" in *Modern Painting* (London: Walter Scott, 1893), pp. 70-83.

[3] Diaz de la Peña (1807-1876), Spanish painter and precursor of Impressionism known for his woodland scenes. See Moore's "A Lesser Light," *The Speaker* (21 March 1891).

[4] Henri Fantin-Latour (1836-1904), French Impressionist painter.

[5] Hercules Brabazon (1821-1906), Paris-born landscape and still-life watercolorist. See Moore's commentary in "The New English Art Club" in *Modern Painting*, pp. 190-212, especially pp. 208-11.

[6] I.e., sixteen years ago. Characteristically, Moore is not factually accurate.

on the matter on which you urgently need enlightenment, nor would a mere appearance in the very flesh assure you that your feelings were valid: all the senses together are necessary for conviction — sight, speech, hearing, touch and smell.

You are a pretty woman, my dear Baronne, and what is more precious in my eyes, you are an instinctive woman. I do not think you have any idea how charmingly your letters read, they chatter like an impulsive brook and transport me whither nature murmurs her irregular rhythms. Ah what I write is but literature — I should not have written that last sentence. Dear pretty woman send me the large photograph at once and I will write at once for a copy of *Les Confessions* — you can rely on me. I never break my promise. I hope the book will please you. I hope it will not destroy your illusion. It will tell you that I was born in Ireland in 57 [i.e., 52], in a great Georgian house on a pleasant green hill, overlooking a long winding lake. It will tell you that my life was lived in Paris and in London. I have never been married.

Always sincerely yours,

George Moore

I have written a long letter and seem to have said nothing but you manage to say a great deal in your letters. How do you do it? You have lived in lovely castles and convents. How I hate convents. *The Untilled Field* told you that. There are some good things in that book I think. You will like it better when you take it up six months hence. It is a dry book and does not claim one's affections at once. The old woman who puts up a window in her church and hears the painted saints singing is intended to represent Ireland.[7] "The Wild Goose" is being translated into German.[8] I have refused permission to translate my books so often that I at length yielded — I don't know why. The woman who is translating it lives in Vienna perhaps that is why.[9]

---

[7] Biddy M'Hale in "Some Parishioners," in later editions titled "The Window."

[8] The only published German translation of "The Wild Goose" is "Die Wildgans" by Clara Barth and Max Freund (Leipzig, 1922).

[9] Brief excerpts of this letter are inaccurately transcribed in Hone's *Life*, pp. 246-47.

Letter 6

Moore to Gabrielle

13 December [1903]
4 Upper Ely Place
Dublin

My dear Baronne,

Your letter has been following me about some time but it has at last run me to earth. "Run to earth" is a hunting expression but you who know English so well will probably understand. You have not told me how you learnt English. Have you been in England? I suppose not or you would have mentioned it. Did you then learn English — to write English fluently in Austria? You speak English I suppose perfectly. Your gift of using the language fluently and originally is your own. It is a pure gift and I enjoy it. You run on, page after page just as one talks and to write as one talks is the best kind of writing. I have never met anyone who could do this like you. Perhaps I am wrong to mention it for now you will be self conscious and some of the charm will fade.

I am cross with you! You should not have sent to Paris for *Les Confessions*. I had intended to send you the book from here. I have not seen the book for many years and have forgotten it. I only remember that I used to like its gaiety and youthfulness. The other day a friend mentioned that it contained in germ the idea of *Esther Waters*. For some time I could not understand what he meant. He explained that the interest and sympathy that the lodging house servant kindled in me was the idea that eventually grew into Esther.[1] I suppose he is right. I am cross with you for having written for this book. I should have liked to have sent it to you but this is not my only complaint. You say I must not hope to be your lover. I confess I had not indulged in much hope that such a consummation might be my good fortune but I am nevertheless disappointed to hear that I may not hope. If you were making a declaration before the Lord Mayor it could hardly be more emphatic and the limitation you place on yourself causes me to see you in a somewhat different light. You see my women, and you confessed yourself one of them, are delightfully frank with their persons, only Evelyn is touched by scruples and her scruples proceed from an excess of passion; hers is a sort of inverted sensuality which turns on itself and denies itself. If Christ were to meet

[1] At the end of *Confessions of a Young Man*, Moore returns to London and lives in a lodging house in the Strand, where "Emma" is the servant. His naturalistic treatment of the character foreshadows his treatment of Esther Waters.

30

Evelyn Innes he would admire her but if he were to meet Sister Teresa[2] he would say *ceci est ma faute*. Chastity is a mean vice and I hope you do not labour after it. You speak of a man who comes to see you and you talk so much about me to him that he goes away jealous. This sounds like a lover. Dear dear Baronne remember we are here for enjoyment — man's fear of enjoyment is perhaps original sin. "Would'st [i.e., Wilt] thou [yet] take all, Galilean, but these thou shall not take, The laurel, the palms and the p[a]ean, the breast of the nymph[s] in the brake." You do not know our great poet Swinburne . . . I must send you the songs and Ballads.[3] I wish I could remember the next verse. "Breasts more soft than the dove's and kindled [i.e., that tremble] with tenderer breath And all the wings of the loves and all the joy before death." I wonder if that is it. It sounds right or very nearly. "And all the joy before death" — Is not that splendid? Say it to yourself when you lie in bed tonight: "Breasts more soft than the dove's and kindled with tenderer breath, And all the wings of the loves and all joy before death." When you come to the word "loves" pause and looking through the darkness of the room whisper — "and all the joy before death." Swinburne brings English poetry to a close a magnificent full close. We are poets as you are musicians. In the same poem he says "Though before [thee] the throned Cytherean be fallen and hidden her head [Yet] thy kingdom shall pass, Galilean, thy dead shall go down to thee dead." Maybe Swinburne's pealing paganism will shock you and you may delay to write to me. How shall I live when you cease to write to me and that will happen one day. But today I look forward with eagerness to hearing from you and to receiving your large photograph. I am here till the spring. In the spring I shall finish my new story *The Lake*. This story interests me enormously. A firm of German publishers want to bring out translations of my novels[4] but translations are so badly written that I

---

2 *Sister Teresa*, the companion novel to *Evelyn Innes*, was first published in 1901. The double novel chronicles the life of religion-haunted Evelyn from her years as a sensuous young woman to her decision to become a nun and her life in the convent.

3 These lines and those that follow are from Swinburne's "Hymn to Prosperpine" (lines 23-26; 73-74) in *Poems and Ballads* (1866).

4 Egon Fleischel & Company of Berlin brought out German translations of *Esther Waters* in 1904 (by Annie Neuman-Hofer), *Evelyn Innes* and *Sister Teresa* in 1905, and *Memoirs of My Dead Life* in 1907 (the latter three by Max Meyerfeld). Meyerfeld (1875-1952), a German scholar and translator, was for many years Moore's main liaison with German publishers. According to Hone (pp. 279-80), Meyerfeld supervised the production of *Esther Waters* and *Evelyn Innes*, but Moore's suspicion that his texts were being tampered with eventually led to a disruption of their relationship.

hesitate. The translator puts German words in place of English words; he does not — I should have said she does not — for translators are generally women — think that she must rethink the book in her own language. The difficulty is that for a translation to be good it must be at once literal and idiomatic. Can you write German prose. If you can send me a translation of one of my short stories, one of the stories in *The Untilled Field*. Dear Baronne write to me soon and believe me to be very sincerely yours,

George Moore

Letter 7

Gabrielle to Moore   [mid-December 1903]

Dear Mr. Moore,

The book[1] has come at last and you don't know how very amazed I was at first! I simply cried. It seemed so horrible that you had been like that and that I hadn't known before and had written to you dear, kind, tender little *lettres*. I had sleepless nights again and I realy felt rather miserable. But now it's all over again. I have read the book a second time and was not shoked any more. I think I like it already for it is so beautifully written and so very, very interesting. But have you realy been like that? How different we are! I always say that I should invent marriage if it had not been invented long ago. And I have been so eager to have children. I have been making *neuvaines* (you don't know how many) and taking cures and doing all that is required. And I am not cruel, no certainly I am not. Of course I very often offend people, sometimes even mortally — my temper is not very good — but when I think of it I have a great wish to be kind to everybody. And if I don't marry again (I have to become a widow first) I shall be a nurse and tend the sick — you will see.

I see you have known real ladies. The one who has written that *lettre*[2]

---

[1] *Confessions d'un Jeune Anglais.*

[2] Gabrielle is referring to the chapter entitled "Extract from a Letter" in *Confessions of a Young Man*. Moore did not identify the woman who supposedly wrote the letter. (See Susan Dick's variorum edition [Montreal and London: McGill-Queen's University Press, 1972], p. 246, n. 1.) In this paragraph Gabrielle also refers to Moore's *appartement* in Paris at the Rue de la Tour, extravagantly furnished and including a large python ("that dreadful beast"). The *"femme de 30 ans"* in the next paragraph is a reference to Chapter V in *Confessions* where Moore expresses his fascination both with the thirty-year-old woman and Balzac's story "La Femme de Trente Ans."

must have been charming. But you call her *bornée* and I am afraid you liked *cocottes* better. And the serpent! I am not *affectée* — it's just the thing I am not — but I could not have come to see you [at] Rue Tour des Dames (or what?) *à cause de* that dreadful beast. Poor little *cochons Indes* — I like them. *Meerschweinchen* we call them and they are so nice and harmless and have new *petits* every week (without any *neuvaines*.) I think you have changed a great deal, have you not, dear Mr. Moore? I hope you will tell me in your next *lettre* that you are married now and I will think of you in the *caractère* and it will amuse me so much! You have 7 children I know and there will be another one next Easter. And you *like* to share the room of your wife's — such an idea *de se vanter de n'avoir jamais passé une nuit avec une femme!* Then you don't know how lovely they are when they wake in the morning. Poor Mr. Moore!

You don't speak so much about *musik* as I expected you would in that book. Perhaps you were not yet so interested in *musik* at that time? You see, you have changed. But then perhaps — and this fills me with horror — you are no more as fond as you used to be of the *femme de 30 ans?* Such a malchance! Just when I am beginning to be one in the full sense of the word. You don't know, I have so much aplomb now and experiences and some tiny little wrinkles about the eyes. But don't think that I am sorry! I like them because they remind me of lots of things — that I have cried and laughed well and loved more than women in general, that I have *lived* my life (this I have stolen to you) and not only *dreamed* it (this is my own invention.) Please tell me in your next letter if you have changed in that respect. Don't forget. If you are fond now of very young women, mere childs, I shall send you a fotograf on which I am in a low dress. I look like 17 when I am in a low dress — it is almost a disgrace. And when you see me you will not be disappointed immediately because one always notices first the childish round face and the rosy cheeks. My voice too is very soft and girlish.

I know you have a great many things to do. You don't write to me very often but I *dye* to know more about you. It's not better, it is worse since I read the book. Write to me sometimes. Are you very rich again? I hope with all my heart you are. I tried to make out your age — I think it's about 55 but I am not sure. Are you more than 55? Don't mind to tell me. I once had a friend who was 69.

I know how it is! I should *hate* you (perhaps) if you had send the book but as you didn't I like you better still than before. Yes, I think it is so. You had sorrows and disappointments — sometimes you feel sad. Please think of me when you do. I want to be your true little friend.

The Untilled Field is very clever and interesting. But I don't think that I could be happy in Ireland. Don't stay there. Come to Austria for a whole year, *do*. I am not here very long. I have not yet very interesting friends but my cousin has. She will introduce them to you. My cousin has *le feu sacré* and a lovely mouth. But she is a girl and can't understand your books as well as I do and ought not to pretend she does. *N'est-ce-pas?* Has she written to you too? She writes like T H A T and her name is MARIETTA. You see, I have not *le feu sacré* just now. I couldn't afford to have. I am *aux petits soins* with my nerfs (the poor little darlings.) I want to sleep soundly every night and I shouldn't if I went to operas and concerts. I want to grow fater, I want a little *matelas* and a soft warm little coverlet for each of my nerfs. This is my ideal at present. No, I don't think that we are here for enjoyment. And I don't think *you* do. But you wish it were so. Well, so do I.

When you come I shall show to you my "Journal." I think it will amuse you. It is written in German, of course, but you know German. You ask how I learned to write English fluently. I don't know. I knew French before I knew German but English I have begun very late. I was 16. And I hated my teacher and could not bring myself to speak to her. But English books very soon interested me. I hardly can speak at all — it *is* funny. Conversation is not my force, perhaps, in any language. I say good things very often, of course, but I say them in a hasty nervous little way and I hate long phrases. Don't you? But I always liked to write. I wrote very nice French letters to my sister when I was 10 and in the convents I had *des prix de style* if of nothing else. I am very busy now with an embroidered waistcoat but after Christmas I shall try to translate a little story. I don't think it is a happy idea to translate *The Untilled Field. Etwas* was so intensiv in Ireland *spielt, in's Deutsche übersetzen. Pfui,* Mr. Moore, *sie können gut Deutsch und ich muss nicht so plagen!* Has any of the ladies — written to you? I forget to tell you — Marietta calls herself *Frau S.* but she isn't a *frau*, it's only because she is a *chanoinesse*. I rather like the English woman who gives me lessons now. I bring her some flowers sometimes and *bonbons*. But the *bonbons* I eat myself on second thoughts. As you say, I am *gourmande*. She doesn't approve of my pronunciation but doesn't think me *quite* hopeless. Dear Mr. Moore, I shall write once more before Christmas but to-day I must stop. I am so busy. I hope you will send your next photograph and don't be disgusted with mine. I assure you I *am mieux*. My colours are lovely, you know. Last night I was dreaming of you and I always know the day before a letter from you is coming. Oh, and when I red the *Confessions* I at once thought that Emma gave you the idea of Esther. Am I not clever? I think I am and besides I love you so.

G.

Letter 8

Gabrielle to Moore   20 Decembre [1903]

Dear Mr. Moore,
    If I had a pretty photograph I should have send it long ago, of course, but I haven't any pretty one and my secret hope has been you would forget all about it. I always look dreadful and *affectée* or swollen and greedy on photografs. I am much *mieux que* this. I don't look so tooth-achish in reality.
    Dear Mr. Moore, I hope you have not been very cross with me, have you? I know it wasn't quite nice of me to send for the book. But I have made excuses at once, have I not? To-morrow I will burn the *Confessions* and you then will send me new ones. Will that do? I am sorry, of course, that my ideas are different with yours but I don't think it is my fault and that we could quarrel about that. I am always changing a little but I couldn't suddenly change *ganz und gar* — I never heard anyone could. I am frank, Mr. Moore, but you see I am a funny little *mélange* of p . . . . and the reverse.[1] It puzzles my best friends but I can't help it. I wonder if you guess the word — it's a French word and means something very nice but I preferred not to write it fully. I don't know why. One of my friends said the other day he never knew a lady who talked so dreadful things as I do but whose eyes looked so innocently all the while. He said my eyes were like a child's.

---

[1] In response Moore (in Letter 12) declined to write the word but suggested it was a "horrid" word. In Letter 13 Gabrielle strongly denies that the word is "naughty" and claims that it is "a *nice* word I meant, a word one often sees in prayer books." We can do no more than guess, but it seems plausible that the word that occurred to Moore was *putain* (whore) when in fact Gabrielle may have had the opposite in mind: perhaps *pucelle* (virgin) or *pudicité* (prudery).

35

I love the little verses in your letter. I always loved and shall love always beautiful things. But course vulgar ones I *hate*. I have always been like that. I remember when I was a little girl of 6 or 7 I was very fond of the *"bibliothèque rose"*[2] but some of the pictures shoked me dreadfully. Mme. Fichiné[3] falling *à la renverse* and exhibiting her dreadful *mollets* was too much for me. I took the book in a corner *pour effacer* the shoking things with a *Radiergummi*. I am not trying to copy Evelyn but I have scruples sometimes. You don't know how pious I have been, how hard I tried to be good and convert the men I liked. If I had been Sir Owen's mistress I sometimes would have pintsched him till he had made an *acte de contrition*. I would have liked to pintsch him to the purpose (but I am afraid he would not have liked it, for there are different ways of pintsching.) My passion to convert men is perhaps what you call a sensuality making pirouettes. No, you expressed it with more dignity. You said a sensuality turning on itself. Here I send to you a letter I wrote nearly five years ago. I was dreadfully in love with that Count H. but I struggled against the feeling and I so wanted him to marry merely to save us both. I don't think that we are here for enjoyment only. I should like to think so but I can't as long as there are beggars, cripples, idiots and sick people without any possibility to enjoy their lives. I *tried* to enjoy myself. There was a moment I could not struggle longer. I will tell you more about my life. Very soon after my marrying C. von H. I fell in love with H.H. (it was not a practical arrangement — do you think so?) I loved him dearly but I simply didn't know at that time that a married lady can have a lover. He made rather tame love to me. I tried to convert him, that was all. You will say it wasn't much? Well, it was enough to give me a taste of happiness and the feeling that I couldn't live without love (what pure thing it meant to me then.) Two years later my husband was send to Prague. I went there too but H.H. could not come, so I rather soon fell in love with another man. I loved him in a violent fashion, O, *how* I loved him, Mr. Moore! I had hot fingertips the moment he entered my room. We met constantly in society. He was giving charming little entertainments himself. He was married and I adored his wife and his 3 little children. His wife expected a baby. I used to sit with her for hours, watching her, giving her little

[2] A series of children's books, particularly for girls, teaching what is socially proper. The books were bound in pinkish covers.

[3] A character from *Bibliothèque Rose*.

hints how to please her husband. In the theatre I knew the moment he entered the Club Loge, though I was sitting on the opposite side in the Latthalters Loge. I didn't *see* him, I am so *myope*, but I *felt* him. And when summer had come we sat together in a large, beautiful garden full of roses and jasmins, holding each other's hands, looking into each other's eyes. You don't know, Mr. Moore, you don't know. He is in Brasilien now. He had dreadful debts — he damaged his best friends. He had *lied* to us. Nobody had suspected, it came so suddenly. He was a *Rasengeschichte*. He nearly lost his title and had to leave at once. He not even dared to bid me good-bye. He made his little boy write a letter to me and he was gone. I only had kissed him twice and I know I should have died if I had been his mistress. As I had not been I went on living but don't ask me how. I flirted with other men just to forget my darling F. It was my first great sorrow but it wasn't the last.

I am telling you all about me. Do you like it, Mr. Moore? I hope you do. But please don't show my letters to anyone. Of course if your wife sees them and says "Dear Georgie, show me that letter please," you must do it. I should be sorry to sow discord in your *ménage*, but don't show them to your friends. It will be tempting perhaps in a way but I should hate the idea. I hope you understand. And tell me please about Grania.[4] Are you making operas too? not only books! I think you are a *unheimlich* clever man.

4 Moore had been trying to convince his friend Elgar to write an opera on the Irish mythological character of Grania. See *ELT*, 21:3 (1978), 168-87 for Eileen Kennedy's "George Moore to Edward Elgar: Eighteen Letters on *Diarmuid and Grania* and Operatic Dreams." Moore of course collaborated with Yeats on the play *Diarmuid and Grania*, which was presented by the F. R. Benson Company at the Gaiety Theatre in Dublin on 21 October 1901.

Letter 9

Gabrielle to Moore   Sunday [20 Decembre 1903]

Dear, dear Mr. Moore, (this is a new *lettre*, you know)[1]

What a charming, delicious letter you have written to me! I am so happy you don't know. And so there is a real Sir Owen and you are great friends with him and you know (how do you know?) that I use to

1 This letter was presumably enclosed with Letter 8 and written just after Gabrielle received Letter 5.

cross my legs. I am in love, in deep love with your dear, dear letter. I took it under *mon oreiller* last night and when I look into it I hear sweet *musik*. You are 46. It is very young. Why do you make as if you were a *vieillard*? I know now that we shall meet. I always had a presentiment and a great, great wish of it, but it's only since yesterday that I am quite sure. When you come to Vienna I will show you the place where it occurred to me. It was in Belvedere as I walked through it towards evening. Your letter was *cachée* in my *manchon* and I was smiling so radiantly that the lady who was with me noticed it at once. But I have something to say to you and I will do it without delay (one has so much *aplomb* sometimes.) Please listen to me but neither laugh nor frown at me. You will not be my lover, dear Mr. Moore, no, *never*. I don't want you to be. Don't think I do. But if I am a widow in a few years I shall propose to you! Yes, this I will. And you won't refuse me perhaps and we shall live somewhere rather far away and I at least shall be so happy. You will write a new book every year and the books will make you famous. I shall have a new b . . . every year and the b . . . s will keep me quiet. I like to be quiet, it suits me. But somehow I am not always and my friend (the one, you know, who came to see me two weeks ago) is afraid that I should grow too insolent, *übermütig*, you know, if I were too happy (that is the reason perhaps he doesn't make me quite happy.) Please don't forget to send the photograph. You will have mine for Xmas.

And so you like my letters? I am so glad, Mr. Moore. I shall write often. I long to please you. To-day my cousin asked me about your address. I was tempted to say: Hotel d'Albe, Champs-Elysées, but I should have blushed awfully and it's so stupid to blush. So I contented myself to be a little vague and to suggest Br. Tauchnitz[2] (poor Br. Tauchnitz! how he must hate us!) Please dear Mr. Moore if my cousin asks you tell only that I have writtten to you once or twice about Evelyn, that you were rather pleased and have send me the book. Don't say more. I should hate it so much. And don't like her better than me. She plays Wagner beautifully on the piano but she is a girl and rather stout. And when you come you must not let know the others at first, only me. I want to have you all to myself for a week at least. I shall advise you about the hotel (it must be one where they do not know me for I shall come to see you and people are so stupid.) I know you will please me.

[2] Bernhard Tauchnitz, the German publisher who published Moore as part of his Collection of British and American Authors.

You will if you don't look too Frenchy. You see, I don't like the French. They are *guindés* and fussy and their hair is oily. I have so many English heroes. I was 18 when I began to pick them out from Tauchnitz editions. I had Douglas (Lady Noel)[3] Richard Feverel[4] — later on Chandos (Ouida)[5] and a 1000 more. But the French hero is called Maurice, which is Jewish, and he speaks about horses, but I don't think that he realy is fond of horses. French heroes I only can endure when they almost are Valois or Bourbons. And they cannot be now-a-days, can they? (some time ago of course they could very easily.) Please be very English and you will not disappoint me. Young men in Austria when they admire something very much, a hat or a dog, a house or a *Walzer*, a racehorse or a lady, use to say "*Das ist* Picadilly 121." It's nonsense after all, is it not? They ought to say "12 Waterloo Place"! Tell me more about Sir Owen. I hope he has a pretty enough wife? You may tell him that a lady in Vienna is writing to you but you must not say my name. You see, my brothers would dislike it. I am a little afraid of my brothers. Niki espacially is like a kilo of *dynamit*. I am not, but you see I always am in love with someone or something, sometimes too with an idea (but this somehow doesn't proof so satisfactory, does it?) 2 years ago I was reading Tolstoi's *Resurrection*[6] and immediately I had a great wish to change my life. I was in love with renunciation! It was *so* funny, you don't know. My husband's regiment just then was send to Gallicia. They were so sorry, the poor dragons, and all the ladies were grumbling. But I was so happy. I thought it was like going to Siberia. I went as fast as I could. My maid had refused to come with me so I took the cook only and I never shall forget how very bewildered she was. You don't know —————— of course. It's very far — it is nearly in Russia (not quite though.) The funny Polish Jews one sees there! And the dirty little village it is. My husband went on horseback, so when he came at last he found me already *établie*. I had choosen the most dreadful little house

---

[3] Lady Augusta Noel (1838-1902), *From Generation to Generation* (1879), published by Tauchnitz in 1880. The novel chronicled the history of a Scottish family named Douglas.

[4] George Meredith (1828-1909), *The Ordeal of Richard Feverel* (1859), published by Tauchnitz in 1875.

[5] Ouida (Marie Louise de la Ramée) (1839-1908), *Chandos* (1866), published by Tauchnitz in 1871.

[6] Tolstoi's *Voskresen'e* was published in London under the title *Resurrection* in 1900 (translated by Louise Maude).

(almost a cabin) that you can imagine. The dining-room was so small that we couldn't ask any friends. The windows were like little holes. Poor Carl was furious. He wasn't in love with renunciation, you see, and found fault with everything, and I very soon found out that the new life consisted in a great deal more quarrelling than before (and you don't know, you can't know, how much that means.) With Carl I have never been in love. I thought I was at first but it was merely because I wanted to marry and because his eyes were kind and his teeth so nice. Besides it was a Saturday when I saw him first and I thought that the *sainte Vierge elle-même* had troubled to arrange the match. And in my next *lettre* I shall tell you about Prague. Do you know Prague? My own dear Prague! I was so happy there. You don't know how proud I am. I pittied myself very much when I first found out that my marriage had been a mistake. But I never complained. I should have hated to be pitied by others. Besides I pitied him just the same. In my next letter I shall tell you too how I am living now in Vienna. I should like to do it at once but this letter would be too long. I hope it will reach you. I am not very well. I won't go out to-day, and I always am anxious when the servants post my letters. Write again please. Just a few kind words will make me so very happy. But don't make me jealous by writing to Marietta. It's so amusing. I have a married aunt also who likes Evelyn tremendously! If you had wished to write a book for Austrian Countesses espacially, you could not have succeeded better. You see in some respects Austria seems to be like Ireland. They all think that you wished to glorify our religion (Monsignors, confession, convents, espacially!) You know, I did too, at first. Monsignors are very much the fashion but Jesuits are still more. And don't ask me please what happens if a Jesuit is a Monsignor! I am sorry already that I mentioned *Les Confessions*. But if you come to Vienna we will explain that you were a great sinner and were converted afterwards. That will do. We have a proverb, *"Man muss mit den Wölfen heulen"* — howl with the wolves, you know. *Au fond* I am exactly like the others.

Yesterday there was the *ballotage* of my younger brother and I at once have been making vows to secure the situation! Now I shall have to rise very early and to go to mass twice a week till Christmas. I shall hate it so much. But one cannot break his vows. Please, Mr. Moore, could you not be pious too? Just a little, you know, and out of love for me? Try. We could say the same little prayer every day at the same hour, you in Dublin, I in Vienna. The *liebe Gott* will like it I think — he will smile goodnaturedly and stroke his long beard. You know, I hope that he has a very long beard. He may have and ought to, but you were right to put off yours. There is one thing more that I want to explain to you. In Paris and even in London even real ladies are rouging and painting, are they not? *We do not here* — I not, at all events. I am just as *bien lavée* as possible and that's all. Could you not come before spring? My freckles are less visible now and furs are becoming. Good-bye now, or rather good night, my dear, great, tall, splendid, good, kind, wonderful Mr. Moore. I hope you are not bored with me. And don't be angry that I have read the book. It was a little like spying through the keyhole, but I like it now so much. Your sweet letter will sleep with me again. Write soon again to your little friend,

G. v.H.

Letter 10

Moore to Gabrielle   21 December 19[03]
                                      4 Upper Ely Place
                                      Dublin

My dear Gabrielle,

I enclose a letter which I have just received from the German publishers about whom I wrote to you last week. The translation they are going to publish will be detestable but if I stop the publication by refusing to allow them to translate *Sister Teresa* I shall merely lose some money. I am hopelessly entangled. I sold *Esther Waters* and I gave a woman who lives in Breslau the right to translate *Evelyn Innes*.[1] Resistance will merely mean loss of money. So without any definite result I am inclined to accept their offer. But what has all this got to do with you. This much, that yesterday I remembered I had asked you to translate one of the stories in *The Untilled Field* and today I am more anxious than ever that you should do this. The letters you write to me are easily and prettily written — you write easily and prettily and wittingly in English, a language which you know very well but which is not your

---

[1] Breslau is a city southeast of Berlin. The only published German translation of *Evelyn Innes* is that by Max Meyerfeld (1905). Moore frequently alludes in his letters to giving unidentified people the rights to translating his various works (see Gilcher, pp. 55-56), but few of the translations, if ever finished, were published.

native language. In German you write better. I suppose it is more difficult to write German than English but after all it is the mind that writes and you have a gay lively mind very like my own. Your letters are not unlike the *Confessions*. You want something to do. Why not do what I asked you to do last week — translate any one story of *The Untilled Field* or a few pages of *Evelyn Innes*. It is true that I do not know German, but I have a friend[2] — a man of letters who lived many years in Germany — he would be able to talk to me about your translation. He tells me that the translations that have appeared of my books are wretched. I am writing a new story called *The Lake* which I think will be one of my best stories and if you can write idiomatic German prose you will enjoy translating this story.

This letter is all business and literature and not half as nice as the letter you wrote to me about the rain and about your weariness of everything.

Do you know Verlaine's poem[3] — it rains on the roof and it rains in my heart. I wonder how it would be to meet you in Venice in the spring. All my life I have been wanting to go there. You tell me you have been there and would it not be nice to see St. Mark's and the Canals and the many things I have read about you.

Chère Gabrielle au revoir,

George Moore

[2] Probably Kuno Meyer (1858-1919), Professor of Celtic at the University of Berlin and co-founder and director of the Summer School of Irish Learning of Dublin (1903).

[3] Paul Verlaine (1844-1896), "Il pleure dans mon coeur," from *Romances sans paroles* (1874).

Letter 11

Gabrielle to Moore   26 Decembre [1903]

Dear Mr. Moore,

I don't understand your letter. What you do mean by idiomatic German? And why are you so anxious about having your books translated? Is it the money you want or the fame? Is it both? I am so stupid. I not even know if 25 pounds is a great deal of money. Tell me how much it is. Tell me in francs or marks, will you?

Dear Mr. Moore, I admire you awfully, and I should like to help you out of your difficulties but I don't see how I could. I have never translated anything. The other day I tried a little but I didn't like it at all. I think only governesses do it, *pas?* You say I write as one talks. I know I do and in every language. But then I don't speak too beautiful German. Nice people never do in Austria. If I were you I should hate to have my books translated (unless I wanted some money.) You don't know perhaps that nice people in Austria and much more still in Germany are fond of reading English books. It is only the horrid ones who want translations. Could you mind the horrid people? Your books are much too good for them. They would not even care for them besides. It gives me *des crampes* of every kind to think of a *Apotheker* or a *coiffeur* reading *Sister Teresa* on Sunday afternoons. There is another difficulty. I am *so* capricious. I always am beginning things but I generally tire of them very soon. I know one ought not to be like that but has not everyone *ses defauts?* Mr. Moore dear, I wished you had asked other things of me and not that particularly nasty one. You see I have a constant fear to become an old maid now that I am without a husband. A few months ago I have been at a Professor's to inquire if there was any chance of my growing a girl again. He made big round eyes at my question and laughed a good deal. Professors are idiots. But you are not an idiot and you will understand that translating novels would be a great way towards it (growing an old maid.) Be sure to write to me very soon and answer all my questions. I am anxious about you. It is not pleasant to think of you as "hopelessly entangled." I hope it isn't so dreadful *que ça*. Tell me please. I think it is naughty to write with a pencil but I have a cold and am obliged to stay in my bed. We had a nice *"heiligen Abend."* My brother came to spend the evening and we were quite merry eating nice things, playing *Hyawata Marsch* and talking about interesting things. I am so glad my brother likes your books. He is *difficile* but he admires you and thinks you are painting your own life in that of the 2 men, Sir Owen and Ulick Dean[1] — your youth and *le temps de vos splendeurs* in Owen Asher's, and your returning home in Ulick's.

In the beginning I hoped I would not tell to anyone about our correspondence. But my hope proofed vain. I have been telling to 9 people! Is that many? But they only think I admire your books. They don't know I am so fond of you. I have been in Venice 7 years ago on my *voyage de*

[1] One of Evelyn's suitors in *Evelyn Innes*, loosely based, in the first edition, on Yeats and, in subsequent revisions, on George William Russell (AE).

noce, and last spring from 11 till 20 May. I had a *rendezvous* there with my brother, who was on his way home. We had quite a good time. I was so happy. Sitting in a gondola looking at the moon and listening to the *musik* is the loveliest thing on earth. That noisy Italian music would be dreadful elsewhere but in Venice one likes it so much. Have you some friends there? Mr. Penini[2] perhaps (if he is still alive. To tell the truth I don't know much about him.) It would be nice of course to go to Venice again but I don't know if I will have *des Ersparnisse* next spring. For me travelling is rather expensif as I am obliged to take my maid. I am *si maladroite* I am not able to make my hair alone. Do you realy think I want something to do? There are other things besides translating. Send me your measures and tell me your *favorite* colours and I will embroider a lovely waistcoat for you! Is *The Lake* about peasants again? Does perhaps idiom mean jargon? I hope there is a realy nice heroine in *The Lake*. One who takes her bath every morning and who sleeps in a nice bed. Do you know what I hate? When heroines (unless they are cocottes — then they may) sleep in *luxurious* beds. Too much lace in a bed gives one *mal aux ongles* and a toothache when one has realy fine nerves and things with feathers in them are rather disgusting. Soft embroidered linen, a silk *couverture* and a white flanell one is all that is required. Don't call me Gabrielle. I am not a *courtisane*. Do I call you Henri?

I will say a rather rude thing now. I am dreadfully in love again with my other friend. It began yesterday when I was in church. You don't know what funny not at all churchey things I was thinking the whole time or nearly. I had to smile and to blush and almost to hide my face in my muff every few minutes. But I always forget the principal thing! (Could such a person translate books?) My friend who was so disposed to find fault with you *likes Evelyn Innes*. He reads it now and thinks to recognise himself in Owen Asher. That he likes the book in spite of his being jealous is your greatest triumph, Mr. Moore. Please write very soon. Tell me exactly what you want me to do.

Cécile

[2] The context suggests that "Mr. Penini" is a nineteenth-century Italian musician, but since we have been unable to identify anyone with that name, it is possible that Gabrielle means Giacomo Puccini (1858-1924), whose *La Bohème* (1896) and *Tosca* (1900) had recently brought him much attention.

Letter 12

Moore to Gabrielle   24 December [1903]
                                      4 Upper Ely Place
                                      Dublin

My dear Gabrielle,

I hope that writing in this familiar way will not offend you. You write to me familiarly and I should not like all the familiarity to be on your side. Moreover Gabrielle is a beautiful name and I have never known anyone called Gabrielle. It is a pleasure to hear and to write the name.

Your photograph arrived a day or two ago. I can easily understand that you are prettier than your photograph but it tells me what you are like inwardly. I can see that you are a real and not an affected woman and that was what I wanted to know. And nothing but this very photograph "which is not a pretty one" could have told me just what I wanted to know. So you see you did wisely in sending it to me. I feel that I should like to meet you much more now than I did before, for now I feel that I shall be meeting a real person. Until you sent me this photograph and wrote your last letter you were but a shadow — the shadow has begun to substantial [i.e., substantiate?], to quicken.

You will let me know when you write again what you think of my Venetian project. Don't you think that Venice could be a better meeting place than Vienna. I must go to Venice — will you believe me when I tell you that I have never seen Italy? and in Venice we shall meet on neutral ground. Of course you will be very disappointed. Remember my dear Gabrielle what you are going to meet — you are going to meet a middle aged man who spends his life writing books. You imagine the author according to your fancy — you know nothing of his labour, of his searchings, of the cigars smoked over the manuscripts. I might break myself to you through a photograph but you might not write again after seeing my photograph. The only thing I can say in my praise is that I am not a disagreeable person to talk to. I fancy, indeed I am nearly sure that if you do not expect too much you will find me agreeable enough to see in Venice and to walk about with. We shall have pictures to talk about. I have written a book about painting but I have never seen Tintoretto and Veronese[1] *dans leur cadre Venetian*. When the first five

---

[1] Tintoretto, sobriquet of Jacopi Robusti (1518-1594), was an Italian portrait painter of the Venetian aristocracy. Paolo Veronese (1528-1588), sobriquet of Paolo Caliari, was an Italian portrait painter born in Verona. Moore makes several passing references to both painters in *Modern Painting* (1893).

minutes are over I am sure we shall get on very well but the first five minutes will be terrible for me. Worse still will be the waiting for you, and worse than the waiting will be the dressing — the choice of which trousers I shall wear, of the cravat, of the shoes . . . I must talk of something else. You know French as well as English. Do you know what "Gaffe" means. I am afraid my last letter to you asking you to translate something may be defined as "une Gaffe." It was stupid of me to want to drag you into the dusty market place of letters — to make a translator of you Dear Gabrielle whom I want to meet in Venice. It was a shame. But this I will ask you to do, I'll ask you to choose a translator for me. I am sure I get two or three applications a month to translate my books into German, I refuse them all because I am afraid of bad German. No one will be able to advise me on this point so well as you. My thoughts go back to your last letter which I am not answering in any true sense. You ask me if I can guess the French word that you say you dare not write but which you indicate. The word that occurs to me, and the only one that seems to fit the sentence is a horrid word — more horrid to me than to you for I have heard it in familiar conversation; you have learned the word through the dictionary. Tell me have I guessed right. I do not dare to write the word. You are such a daring person — you would write anything or rather you would think anything. Perhaps you are not so daring in body as in mind. I am going to send you Swinburne's poems for a Christmas present. The question raised by me and commented on by you in your last letter — what we are here for whether for our personal pleasure or for the pleasure of a god is a vast one and cannot be treated effectively at the end of a letter. Besides we need leave something for our Venetian conversations which I hope will begin soon.

Dear Gabrielle I am

> Very sincerely yours,
>
> George Moore

Letter 13

Gabrielle to Moore   2 Janvier [1904]
                                                Vienna

Dear Mr. Moore,

Your last letter is so nice and such a comfort! I am very glad indeed that you don't want me to translate your books. It is stupid of course, I

46

know, but I prefer simply to read and to love them. You understand all now — you are a darling, dear Mr. Moore. But I have been ill and feel so weak and cannot write a long letter to-day. I have not eaten too much, which sometimes happens at Christmas, but I had a dreadful cold and no breath at all for a night or 2. I hope we *shall* meet, dear Mr. Moore. When will it be? What month? If I were free to do what I like I should of course go to Venice, but I cannot do what I like, I realy cannot just now. I must be careful. I could not go to Venice alone. I only could go there with my brother or some ladies. Would that be nice for you? I don't think it would, so I ask you again, come to Vienna. Will you? You can go to Italy afterwards. It isn't a grand *détour*. I will tell you exactly how you will do it if you are a dear Mr. Moorel (that "l" *vous laissera rêveur*! but we always put a "l" or "erl" to names and words when we want to be extra nice and tender, and that I will do as long as you don't ask dreadful things of me.) You will not tell your real name in the hotel — you will tell them you are Mr. Dayne[1] from London and as soon as you are rested you will send me a little note in which you will tell me the number of your room and *à quelle heure* you expect me! I then shall come at once. Dear, dear Mr. Moore, how nice it will be. I shall stay an hour and a half, and even if we are a little disappointed we shall laugh a good deal because it *is* amusing when a lady comes to see a gentleman she has not seen before! Have you ever heard of such a funny thing? Tom, my dear naughty little dog, will be there too to help us over the first five minutes. But I am sure your clothes will be all right. If they are a little *à la* Ulick Dean I simply will know that you have other and better things to think of than fashions. A *cravatte* is such a little thing. I very seldom notice a *cravatte*. You must not make apologies — that you are middle-aged is one of your best qualities (I realy don't like young men) and that you write books is your best quality since they are so beautiful. We shall speak so much about Evelyn, *n'est-ce-pas*? The next day we shall meet in a museum, the next in a *fiacre* and we shall take a lovely drive, and the *last* day you shall come to see me. Of course you will stay here as long as you like.

You may call me Gabrielle if you realy like it so much. I shall not be offended. It is my second name. When I was borne they saw at once that I was not a boy and they were disappointed as a son was wanted.

---

[1] Dayne was Moore's original name for the protagonist in *Confessions of a Young Man*, but he changed it to "George Moore" in the 1889 and subsequent editions. He used the name again in *Elizabeth Cooper*.

They called me Gabrielle, for they think in Austria that when a girl is called Gabrielle the next child will be a boy! It is on account of that angel, you know, who brought the message of the Messiah's birth. I don't think that you have guessed the right word. It is a *nice* word I meant, a word one often sees in prayer books. I don't mind the naughty words — it is the nice ones that sometimes are difficult to say. But now good-bye, dear Mr. Moore, and please send me the photograph, will you? I should like so much to know a little what you are like. Don't tease me. I shall not stop to write — *au contraire*, I shall write a long dear *lettre* the moment I have your photograph. Good-bye.

Your

G.

Letter 14

Gabrielle to Moore   12 Janvier [1904]

Dear Mr. Moore,

Thank you very much for your photograph and for the beautiful book. *I realy like your photograph.* I am not disappointed, not a bit. Only you look so respectable; you look very *anstandig*. I no longer shall dare to write to you in that naughty way. Your nose is very long, I think, and your eyes are blue? I don't mind the moustache — it's only beards I dislike. But why don't you write to me? Are you cross with me again? I hope you are not. I shall begin *tout à l'heure* to read the *ballades*. I am so glad to have this book. But I can't write a nice and gay letter to-day. I just wanted to keep my promise to write as soon as I had your photograph. But some visitors are coming. One can never do as one likes. My friend is here, *but Ich habe nicht viel von ihm.* I asked him with some other friends. There is my mother, who does not approve of my seeing men at my house. She is in Vienna now. I met her the other day. I wanted to be nice but she was not nice at all! It is, you see, such an unusual thing to divorce in Austria. I am nearly the only one of the whole lot. I must be so careful and I hate it. This isn't a nice letter — I am in a dreadful hurry. Good-bye, dear Mr. Moore, and thank you for all your kindness. What a clever face you have! I am perhaps a little afraid of you now but not very much.

Yours truly

Gabrielle

Letter 15

Gabrielle to Moore   Jeudi [14 January 1904?]

Dear Mr. Moore,

A friend of my cousin, a not at all young but very clever girl wants to try to translate your books. I told her about your letter and gave her your address. She will write to you I think. I am not jealous of her — you may write to her, but please dear Mr. Moore don't tell her a word about me. She repeats everything to my cousin and my cousin *trätschen* very, very much. They know I have written to you several times and that I am fond of reading your books and that you have send your photograph. But they don't know of course that I have written so dreadful things and that I asked you to come to Vienna (this *espacially* they must not know,) and that we want to marry or not to marry — which is it? I don't remember. I am dreadfully *en l'air ces jours ci.* I am not able to write a reasonable *lettre* but I very often look at your photograph and I like it, I do Mr. Moore. My brother thinks it isn't a real photograph but made after a portrait — is that so?

Good-bye, dear Mr. Moore. Will you never write to me again? I hope Eva I. will translate properly. I know you will like her name. She is a Hungarian and lives with my cousin now. Don't fall in love with her and *surtout* don't make me any *niches.* Be a dear good *verlässlicher* Mr. Moore. Good-bye.

Gabrielle

Letter 16

Moore to Gabrielle   18 January 1904
                                            4 Upper Ely Place
                                            Dublin

My dear Gabrielle,

You see I avail myself of your permission to use your beautiful name and to do so is in accordance with English feeling for here when a woman conceives a wish to kiss a man she no longer writes to him or thinks of him as her So-and-So, whatever his name may be. I am glad you are pleased with the photograph and your brother is right, it is not taken from life but from a picture. The picture was painted last summer and is supposed to be very like me.[1] The nose is too long and the eyes are too far apart but it is nevertheless more like me than a photograph taken from life. It certainly is a little commonplace and respectable, very unlike Manet's celebrated portrait[2] which would frighten you so extravagant is it. Though it were done twenty years ago it is more essentially like me than any other. I hate photographs and never sat [but] once to a photographer and will never sit again. One copy remains. I will have it copied and send you one. As to my delay in writing to you I have only to say that I live in the new story I am writing; I write all day seven eight nine hours and am falling out of health. I can think of you but I find all other writing difficult. This story[3] besets me at every moment of the day very often at night. I shall not recover my natural self until it is finished. I expect to finish it in about a month. And now about the translation question. I confess to an *arrière pensée*. You gave me to understand that you were not very well off and I thought you might like to make some money. You could have had for translating *Sister Teresa* about 1200 francs a little more perhaps. I think I could have got a little more for you. I have sold my German right of the two books *Evelyn Innes* and *Sister Teresa* to the Berlin publisher so there is no use in your cousin writing to me. She came a day after the fair. I know too well how women translate, you I thought might prove the exception. Your question "What do you mean by idiomatic German?" amused me. You asked if it means jargon. Well, not quite. The difference between idiom and jargon is a delicate literary question and I am too weary of literature to

1 Possibly a portrait by Mark Fisher painted in 1903. According to Hone (p. 246), Moore liked the painting more than any other that had been done of him. Fisher (1841-1923) was an American-born painter with whom Moore was a close friend for many years. Moore said Fisher "possesses the sentiment of proportion and the instinct of anatomy" in the 1900 edition of *Modern Painting*, pp. 249-51. It may be a painting by Sir William Orpen, also done in 1903. Orpen (1878-1931) was born in Ireland and trained at the Dublin Art School and the Slade. He was one of the most successful painters of his day, his imagination being more literary than pictorial. For more on Fisher, see C. Lewis Hind, "Mark Fisher," *Art Journal* (London), December 1910, pp. 15-20. For more on Orpen, see Frank Rinder, "William Orpen, R.H.A.," *Art Journal* (London), December 1909, pp. 16-24.

2 A pastel portrait painted approximately 1879, presently owned by the New York Metropolitan Museum of Art. For a concise discussion of this and the two other known paintings of Moore by Manet, see Susan Dick's variorum edition of *Confessions of a Young Man* (Montreal and London: McGill-Queen's University Press, 1972), p. 244, n. 8.

3 *The Lake.*

discuss it. If your cousin writes to me I shall of course not think of telling her about our correspondence. Your naughty letters are charming for they are your self and I hope to receive another before long. You need have no fear that anyone will see your letters so write the thoughts that pass through your mind however "naughty" they may be and I hope they will be very naughty.

Always yours,

George Moore

Letter 17

Gabrielle to Moore   25 Janvier [1904]

Dear Mr. Moore,

   I want to write a nice long letter to you to-day. I was so glad to hear of you again. You had not written for such a long time. I couldn't imagine what had happened to you and I realy was rather anxious. Now I am relieved but only a little, for I am jealous of the new story, and then I am sure that you will die very soon if you go on writing from morning till night. Why do you do it, dear Mr. Moore? Realy I must scold you a little. I don't want you to fall ill. You may write 4 or 5 hours every day but not more. And you must go for long walks. One must walk every day for 2 hours at least. When will the book be printed?[1] I hope Br. Tauchnitz won't loose much time about it. I must write to him and tell him how eager I am for *The Lake*. Do you know what would be nice? To read it together, you with me. But it will not be. Quite nice things never happen. But you have a kind heart, Mr. Moore, and I am glad of it, and I wonder why you don't say so in your *Confessions*. It is nice of you to want me to make some money and of course I should love to get 1200 francs. For 1200 francs I could bye heaps and heaps of flowers and a little wife for Tom [her dog] and some amusing *bric-a-brac*, and I would feel rather proud, I think, for I have never as yet earned anything. There is only one difficulty — I am not sure if it would please *meine Väter*. They would hear of it somehow (this I know) and they would feel uncomfortable in their graves, asking themselves if they had left me

---

[1] Delays and rewriting caused *The Lake* not to be published until 10 November 1905.

so little money and reproaching themselves for it. "*Väter*," you know, means ancestors, for of course even here one cannot have more than one father. I am not rich, you see, in those old families it is but the eldest son who is, and my marriage was a bad marriage *sous tous les rapports*. But I nevertheless am not quite poor, indeed some people think I am rather well off. Living the quiet little life I live I could perhaps save some money but I *don't* as I hate to make calculations, to be *kleinlich*, etc., I think I am like you in that respect. I was so pleased with one passage in your last letter. You tell something about English feelings. I was afraid you wanted to be thoroughly French, with no English feelings whatever. But that would have been a little pose, you know, and I *hate poseurs*. So I am awfully glad indeed. I hope I shall never see "Manet's celebrated portrait." There are a great many good things in you. I feel there are when I read your letters and books and each time I look at your picture. But Paris has spoiled you a little and I am cross with Paris for it. But if you are so fond of the French you will perhaps like to hear that my family was a French family. The name is French. But my ancestors did emigrate 1600 and something (it was for a particular reason but I realy have forgotten what it was) and settled in Bohemia, where they got a beautiful place. The place belongs to Niki now. I have lived there so many years that this little photo ought to interest you. You see, I want *de vous distraire un peu*. You must think of me and not only of your books. You must be fond of me, as fond if not fonder as of your heroines. Are you a little fond of me, Mr. Moore? Would you like to sit near me, to hold my hand and to tell me all your troubles? Tell me please.

One of my friends, a lady living near Aufsburg, wants me to come in spring. I must be here in April, for in April a little nephew (I hope it won't be a niece) is coming, so I probably shall go in March (but before 10th or 12th.) I only write this to you *für den fall* that you are coming to Vienna. It would be too dreadful for words if you came and Gabrielle had left! You never would get consoled, I hope, nor would I. I look everywhere for a funny little thing I wrote when I was 18. It is called "Mon Portrait" and I am sure it would amuse you. But I cannot find it. I never find things when I look for them. Do you? I am a little *fatiguée* to-day, a little subdued. I have a *langen, weiten Schlafrock* on and I look rather pretty. I should like you to be here to-day. I should like to have tea with you. There are a great many things I should like to ask you about. Were you realy a little pleased when I first wrote to you. What was your first idea about me? I never, never, never shall forget what great impression your first letter made on me. I got it the 7 *Novembre* on a Saturday. Nearly every year something happens to me the 7 Nov. It is a dangerous day for me. And how can you know so well what a convent is like? You have never been a nun, I suppose. And if you think we are here for enjoyment, why then do you write books that give one a great wish to be good and virtuous? I have done quite a funny thing — when the first time I had read *Evelyn Innes*. I shall tell you one day. To-day I can't. I won't be naughty to-day. You like naughtiness and you will be disappointed, but I can't help it. I promised my friend, you see. I told him in what manner I had written to you and he wasn't pleased at all. Indeed, I think he was *furious*. He has such dear, gentle ways that one never knows. But "*hysterisch*," "impossible," "indecent," were the words he used. Dear Mr. Moore, have I realy been writing quite, quite dreadful things? Tell me please.

Your photograph is before me. I look at it every moment. I like your long, long face and your soft white hair. But we are not a bit alike. My face is so round and my nose is rather pretty but a stupid, short little nose. Dear Mr. Moore, don't write to me long letters if it worries you but think of me as much as you can, and send me please some views (such cards you know) of Dublin. I wonder what Dublin is like? I sometimes think it must be like Prague. Good-bye, and mind the 5 hours at most and the long walks to please your little

Gabrielle

A dreadful thing happened a moment ago. I kissed your photograph!

Letter 18

Gabrielle to Moore   Sunday [31 January 1904?]

Dear Mr. Moore,

I am so glad you wrote to Eva with a *Schreibmaschine* and not in your dear ugly handwriting, which would have been much *plus intime*. It is difficult to read your *lettres* — sometimes it is a little *wiederkunft*, as I told my cousin to-day. But my heart would break, I am sure, if you wrote to me with your *Schreibmaschine*. You must not do it, *never*. I hope you know what a *wiederkunft* means? Not by experience, of course, but *akademisch*, as we say. When I read *Esther Waters* I thought: "*Wiederkommen* is not his force." You hurry through it, you know. You do it without conviction. But I am sure you have improved since then. What do you think, Mr. Moore? Am I again on the verge of naughtiness? I am afraid I am, but my friend *deserves* it: he has provoken me dreadfully. He wrote such a funny *lettre* to me. He likes your books and approves of them, but he thinks I must be very careful in writing to you, as you might do dreadful things with my *lettres*. I not even dare to say what things. I know such things do happen sometimes, but I am sure you are not a scoundrel and I am trusting you with all my heart. I can't help it, you see, and I think I would not if I could, for it gives me so much pleasure to write to you and I am always Oh so happy when a *lettre* from you comes.

Dear Mr. Moore, I like your photograph. It frightened me in the beginning but it doesn't now. I look at it so much. I am glad your hair is white. I am glad you have nice moustaches. It is so fortunate they are not like that ( ) — that would be dreadful. You have what I call a horse face. My face is like a cat's. I wonder if you are as tall as I am. I don't think you are. I am 1 meter and 77. Please don't forget to send me those cards, views of Dublin, you know, with some polite words on them and not the least "Gabrielle." I want to show them to my brother. My cousin left me a while ago. I begin to like Marietta and she likes your photograph. *Eva* is not my cousin, you know. She is a poor girl living at my cousin's now. If you come to Vienna (Mr. Moore dear, why are you not coming?) we shall tell Marietta as soon as the first week is over (I must have you all to myself for a few days, of course.) But afterwards it will be nicer when she knows you are here. She will ask us both for tea or lunch, and *à trois* we could perhaps go to theatres and so. To-morrow I'll send you a card with the name of an hotel on it. The hotel I told you about some weeks ago would be absurd. But will you come? Tell me, please. I don't want to tease you. I only want to know. My friend tells me that you cannot be tender-hearted, as the English never are. Is that true? It may be you are not tender-hearted, but I could make you perhaps. My friend knows how fond I am of fondness. Oh, he is very sly indeed — (the dear old boy, I wonder if you would like my friend?)

I made some little calculations *tout à l'heure*. I think I should have quite enough money to go to Venice in spring. But you see, I could not trust myself to meet you in Venice — indeed I think I could not. I cannot explain why but I hope you will understand. Try please to under-

stand. I never shall forget my first night in Venice last spring. I sometimes am a little *étourdie* and I had lost my maid and my luggage at the
frontière. I had not even a [space left blank] to sleep in. But the bed was
nice and I feeled very happy. I don't think my windows were open — I
think it was too cold for that but somehow I felt the softness of the air
and there was not the slightest noise to be heard except the *bauschen* of
the wind in the canals. It was *delicious*. But I had gone to Venice to
meet my brother and brothers did not strike me as a particular useful
invention that night. I saw lovely statues in Venice. There was espacially
one which I liked to look at — a "Leda with the Swan."[1] Do you like
statues of Leda? I hope you never will expect me to talk clever things
about pictures and statues. I can't do that (and why should I?) I like
beautiful things but I could not say why they are beautiful.

This is such a stupid *lettre* and I am sure I am boring you very much.
I am a little sleepy already but I must tell you a little story before I say
goodnight. You know, I think that my mother is not nice to me. I wrote
you so, I think. She is *à* Vienna a month now or 6 weeks but I have not
yet called on her, as I know she doesn't want to see me. My mother is a
little *extraordinaire* though very nice and grand to look at. But you will
never guess what one of my aunts wants me to do! To call on my
mother's Confessor (a Jesuit of course) to tell him all my troubles, that I
feel lonely, etc, etc, so that he might pity me and try to change the situation. He is the only person they think who has an influence on my
mother. And so the next time she comes to Confession Pater X would
tell her, "My dear lady, for a *pénitence* you must be nice with your
daughter and ask her for tea as soon as possible." I hope he would tell
her too to give me the nicest cakes and plenty of them and no poison
instead of cream. I hope you like my story. These little photos will not
amuse you I fear — they are rather old (they were made in Salizien)
and so badly printed. But this is not my fault. My dear, dear Mr. Moore,
goodnight. Write soon to your very sleepy

Gabrielle

[1] Perhaps at the exhibition known as the Biennale, which had begun in 1895.

Letter 19

Gabrielle to Moore   [early February 1904?]

Dear Mr. Moore,

I have forgotten the little fotographs in my last letter and I send them to-day. I hope you are well and I hope you won't swear at my writing so often now! Do you often swear? I think I like swearing in general. Don't you. I hope you will write to me very soon. It gives me little headaches to wait for a letter. You don't write to me often and I am sure you don't like me at all. I read in a book to-day that the ladies in Ireland are most beautiful, much more beautiful than any other women. Is that true? Tell me please about yourself, about your life. Are you in love with somebody? Is she living with you? I don't think you care for the Dublin ladies. I think you go to Paris when you want to have a good time, to spend money and to make love. Yesterday at the dentist's it occurred to me that perhaps you have false teeth. But you *may* have — I don't mind. I make *des concessions* for you because you have written *Evelyn Innes*. Dear Mr. Moore, do you quite know how wonderful you are? All women ought to be in love with you. But do you know what I did last night? Well, no, I didn't exactly *do* something, but I was thinking of you and it was so nice! Write to me. Don't be cruel. I am spoiling you dreadfully, I know, but I think you like it and I am so kindhearted that I like to give pleasure to others. If you don't come to Vienna we must meet in Munich on my way to my friends. Would you like it? I hope you will write soon to your

Gabrielle.

Letter 20

Moore to Gabrielle   [early February 1904?]
                                      4 Upper Ely Place
                                      Dublin

My dear Gabrielle,

I cannot let the day pass without writing to thank you for the letter which I received this morning. And I should like to write a long letter but I am so tired that I can hardly form a sentence. I do not know why I work so hard. There is no need — I do not depend on my writing for livelihood. I have large estates which I hope the new land act will enable me to sell to the peasants.[1] The negotiations are troublesome and these negotiations together with some pressing literary work will keep me in Ireland till the middle of next month. I shall be in London in March. My friend Elgar[2] — our only musician is having a festival given him, and he would be sorry if I were not present. In the summer I shall go to Bayreuth; I thought I should never go there again, *mais il ne faut jurer de rien.* Your guesses are not altogether right. My hair is not white but one lock in front is white or very nearly. My teeth are well enough but I broke one when I was at school and have had to wear a false tooth all my life. Cricket is a dangerous game. The ladies here are not desirable and my love affairs have happened in Paris and London. Some of them were delicious and I have every reason to believe that I acquitted myself honourably. I am friends with them all so you need have no qualms about your letters. One should never refrain from pleasure and you say that you refrained. Was the thought of me really sufficient. I wish I had been by you — you great tall Gabrielle. Do not think that I am losing interest in you. I look forward to seeing you, to admiring you and to ———. You can fill up the blank with the word you prefer, several will be equally true.

Always dear Gabrielle yours

George Moore

You do not know why I came to live in Ireland. The enclosed[3] will tell you. It was written three years ago.

---

[1] There were a number of "land acts," the first instituted by Gladstone in 1870. However, Moore is doubtlessly referring to the Land Purchase Act of 1903, which allowed the state to help tenants buy out landlords.

[2] Sir Edward Elgar (1857-1934) composed the celebrated funeral march for Diarmuid's death at the end of Act III of *Diarmuid and Grania.*

[3] Possibly "A Plea for the Soul of the Irish People," in *The Nineteenth Century and After,* February 1901. First printed as "The Irish Literary Renaissance and the Irish Language" in *The New Ireland Review,* April 1900. It is the address Moore gave before the National Literary Society at a luncheon 22 February 1900 at the Gresham Hotel, Dublin, as one of the events of "Irish Literary Theatre Week." The text was also printed 23 February in *Freeman's Journal,* and slightly abbreviated in the Dublin *Daily Express* and paraphrased in *Irish Times.*

Letter 21

Gabrielle to Moore   10 February [1904]

[no salutation]

"*Un grand garçon roux! Roux?* You are *roux?* Thank you, dear Mr. Moore, of being *roux.* It is no disgrace, of course, to have red hair. My father had and some people think I have myself. But you could have told me at once, before I had fallen in love with your *white* hair. He said a great deal more but he said it *si vite, si vite* — I realy could not understand. It had been a sudden inspiration — but I think I had better explain.

Yesterday when I was waiting at the *dentiste* I read in the newspapers that Catulle Mendès[1] was in Vienna. I remembered at once that you were friends with him in Paris, and though I was very sorry to disturb him I knew I would ask him about you — through the telefon. I did so the moment I had made out in what hotel he was staying. I didn't give him my real name — I think one must not in such cases. *Un grand garçon roux!* Is not that very amusing? It was a long time till he understood what I wanted to know. I didn't know how to express myself and I had forgotten all my French in the excitement. He said something about *un livre.* I hope you are not cross with me? You see, it was an inspiration, and I am rather proud of it because I don't think many people have inspirations when they are waiting for the *dentiste.*

I now read a German book about Ireland. They say in it that to live a happy life in Ireland one must be a lord, a tree, or a cow. They forget the saints in their niches. But I would not be happy if I was an Irish saint in a beautiful golden shrine because I know you would not come to say prayers at my feet — you don't like me. Good-bye, dear Mr. Moore.

G.

---

[1] Catulle Mendès (1843-1908), French poet, novelist, and playwright. Moore had met Mendès in Paris during the 1870's.

Letter 22

Gabrielle to Moore   [mid-February 1904]

Dear Mr. Moore,

Thank you 1000 times for your dear kind *lettre*. I received it this morning and it made me so happy. I like you better every day. You are so nice and *sympatisch* on the little picture in the old newspaper. I had no time yet to read the article properly, but I will do it to-morrow. You are rather naughty indeed in your last letter! But I am not too much shoked. Perhaps I am not at all. I don't know. Catulle Mendès has a *Vortrag* about Wagner this evening. I shall go, but I shall not understand if he *parle si vite* again. 4 years ago I read one of his books and there was such a very disgusting description of an old Jew that I couldn't eat anything for 1 day or 2. I am very cross with him for it but I didn't tell him so.

My dear Mr. Moore, *ne vous fâchez pas* if I say good-bye already. The weather is so lovely to-day that I must go out for a long, long walk. I shall try to think of you again. If you come to Vienna will you *halten* a *Vortrag* too? About what? Enjoying's one life? And never refraining from pleasure? But then they will be obliged to have the lights *ausgelöscht*. I am so sorry, I have been writing on a wrong sheet of paper but I realy have no time to copy it all over again. You must forgive me. Will you? Do tell me — have you sometimes 2 mistresses at the same time? I know a man who has and I should love to know if it is quite a usual thing. Please don't like anyone better than me. I realy think I should be jealous.

Your loving

Gabrielle

"Loving" Gabrielle — that is not *too* tender perhaps? I am not sorry, you know, about the red hair. I only wanted to tease you, and I am neither sorry about your false tooth. I am glad you played criket when you were a boy.

Letter 23

Gabrielle to Moore   20 [February 1904]

Dear Mr. Moore,

For more than an hour now I have been studying the calendar, a large map and the *Kondukteur* — the book, you know, where one finds the trains. I am very clever at looking them out now, for a friend teached me. You see, friends are useful. But is "teached" *richtig*? I am afraid it is not, but to-day you realy must not tease me, for I am been in bed 2 days and I am still a little weak. I even had *un peu de fièvre*, and I think it was *d'avoir trop penser à vous*! My head is full of plans and I must tell them to you — *es lasst mir keine Ruhe*. I want to see you soon and you realy could come to Munich, Regensburg or Nuremberg. My friend is living between Aufsburg and Regensburg — Nürnberg is only an hour beyond Regensburg, so if you don't prefer Munich I could go there. It is the same to me. An hour doesn't make a great difference. Nürnberg is so pretty. It realy is not far from London if you take *den Vig über Ostende, Koln.* Of course, if you come *über* Paris it takes much longer, for then one stays in Paris a fortnight or more! Dear Mr. Moore, will not your book be finished soon? I thought about the end of this month. And what about that "festival" given to your friend? A festival lasts a day or 2 — it doesn't last *weeks* (unless it is a Jewish festival.) Let us fix a day at once. The 12th or 13th of March would suit me best. *Sontag lätare — das ist das wahre*, though I am not a *Schnepfe.* Don't you think it would be a good day? Then there is the 24th — St. Gabriel — almost my fête! Would you not like to be nice to me that day? to tell me that I am not only an angel but an archangel? Mr. Moore, dear Mr. Moore, think about it and tell me soon please if you like my plans. You would arrive in the morning, I towards evening as I hate to travel in the night. We could not stay at the same hotel, but as soon as I am a little rested and tidied (you will have the *whole* day to rest) I will let you know and we shall pass the evening together — I don't know where, perhaps in the theatre in the background of a box, not listening to the play but chattering and looking at each other, and the next day you shall have me from morning till evening. I'll rise extra early if you want it. But my complexion is not nice after a journey — my skin is so delicate. You don't hate to travel I hope? You see, I think it would be better even for you to see me soon before you come to Vienna. Vienna is farther than Munich, and you ought to know before you come till there, *si vraiment j'en vaux la peine*. No, it is not that. It is simply I think that I won't wait any longer. I am not ashamed to run after you, but I very soon will be ashamed of thinking so much of a man without even knowing if he deserves it. It makes me feel what I don't want to be: *a little fool*. Dear Mr. Moore, write to me — tell me if you like my plan.

[no signature]

Letter 24

Gabrielle to Moore   [early March 1904]

Dear Mr. Moore,

I did not go to see Catulle Mendès. I merely wrote to him a few lines, and he was kind enough to answer *"poste restante."* I thank you for your last letter and for the *Pall Mall Magazine*. I like the "Avowals"[1] and I like the smell of the paper. But I certainly don't like the story of the Duchess.[2] It is a horrid story and I hope not a true one? I hate disgusting things and I think I told you so a long time ago. Please mind it for the future. Good-bye. I am a little stupid sometimes but I like me to be like that. I have been crying, my nose is swollen and I have hardly any eyes. I am like the ladies of Dublin to-day — not desirable! I will not write a nice letter to-day. You don't deserve it I think.

Yours truly

Gabrielle v. H.

Do tell me please that you invented the story or that you had a little *"Schwips"* that Sunday afternoon. Do you know what a *"Schwips"* is? Ask your German friend. He has some too sometimes I am sure.

[1] Chapters IV-XI of *Avowals* (1919) were published in *Pall Mall Magazine*, March through August 1904.

[2] Possibly an anecdote related by Moore in an earlier, missing letter.

Letter 25

Gabrielle to Moore   14 [March 1904]

Dear Mr. Moore,

Now I know all about you. You are *un aimable compagnon d'une
élégante allure, parlant bien le français et écrivant de bons livres dans le
goût naturaliste* (?) and you are *agréable* and a *poète distingué* and a
parfait galant. Is that enough? Or are you anything more? Dear Mr.
Moore, I am so happy. The weather is lovely — it is spring already I
think. The air is smelling of *tulipes.* It is delicious and I have been to
confession. I had such a beautiful drive in the beautiful Schwarzenberg-
garten in a *Kutschirwagen.* The old *fürstin* was driving herself, and it
was so, so nice. I am friends with one of the young princesses, her
daughter-in-law, and she has come to Vienna now for the birth of her 5th
child and I am so glad. She is so nice. But I think every woman ought to
bear a child in spring, and I despise the women who don't even if they
could. I don't care for dirty little boys, but I am so fond of pretty little
girls. I have been to the theatre with Marietta and the play was good
and it made me cry. And I must stop now because you are busy with
your book and don't want to be disturbed, and because my pen is horrible. But I think to write untidily is rather a sign of genius, is it not? So
everyone should take care to write untidily and *surtout* to omit all the
points sur les "i's." Marietta is a little *piquée* that you are so long in
answering to her letter, but Siegfried Wagner is in Vienna now. She likes
him very much. And you did not jump out of pleasure that I proposed
to meet you in Munich! Well, you are funny Mr. Moore. I ought to go
soon to be here again soon after Easter, but I sometimes am so funny
and cannot *fassen einen Eutschluss.* Good-bye, dear Mr. Moore. You
must not think that Gabrielle is a rare name here. I know 13 Gabrielles.

                        Gabrielle

Letter 26

Gabrielle to Moore					25 Avril [1904]
							Vienna

Dear Mr. Moore,
    I am in such a mood for letter-writing to-day and I see so many green
things from my windows that it makes me think of Ireland. Vienna is so
lovely now. Where are you? Still in Dublin? Or have you a *rendezvous*
with Marietta? She is in Italy. Write to me (quite a short letter will do)
where you stay now and I'll send you a new photograph of Gabrielle. I
wait and wait for your new book but it doesn't come. As an author you
will always interest me. I cannot help to admire your books and some of
your letters were very charming too. I am here till the beginning of June.
Will you write a little letter to me? That new photograph will please
you I hope. I am well. I am so reasonable now, *too* reasonable I think.
I don't know how long it will last!

							Sincerely yours

							Gabrielle

Letter 27

Moore to Gabrielle					23 June [1904]
							Hotel Continental
							Paris

My dear Gabrielle,
    I arrived here on Friday, no, on Sunday morning and when I came
down from my room your letter was handed to me. The coincidence is
startling. You had not heard from me for months — forgive me, dear
Gabrielle. I could not write, I intended to many times; something inspired you to address a letter to me in Paris and the letter and I arrived
together eight o'clock on Sunday morning. I crossed by New Haven and
Dieppe. The photograph you speak of in your letter reached me this
morning forwarded from Dublin, and it has given me so much pleasure
that I feel I must write to you at once. But I haven't your address. You
forget to write your address and however often I might copy it I should
forget it. I cannot remember the names of German streets: I am forced
to send this letter to your photographer with instructions written by the

Hotel clerk to forward it. The photograph is deliciously like you; I can see that though I have never seen you — the photograph is so personal and you are so personal so entirely yourself. Your head is admirably set on the shoulders and your hair is thick — you tell me it is fair hair — nothing is more beautiful than thick fair hair. And I like the tender earnest expression in your eyes and your thin delicate figure. I divine its tender gracefulness through the stays — you do not require stays — and though you are thin I am sure one would not come across a bone while looking for a contour. It is a great pity you are not in Paris. The weather is beautiful and it inspires love; the delicious Aphrodite awakes me every morning and all day she is by me — it is a pity you're not here Gabrielle. I could love you. I understand so well, so well what you mean when you say that life is dry and empty when one hasn't a lover. It is extraordinary how perfectly you express yourself, so easily and so accurately, conveying your mood; your letters are full of you, of the beat and persuasion of your very young person. We're in the middle of Love's season. The divine sense of union is the greatest joy . . . But Gabrielle I am going back to Ireland to write books. I do not know why I am going. I only know that I am going; an instinct drives me. I wish Aphrodite would send me to Munich for it would [be] enchanting to meet you there. But if I were to go I should lose my chance of finishing *The Lake* and writing a comedy that tempts me.[1] You are better than literature, I know. I can see that you are a dear woman. Your photograph tells me all about you. I appreciate you Gabrielle and do you not judge me by my letters. They are often written lightly even factitiously. There is a better side and I have not shown it in my letters to you. If we were to meet you would like me better but if we were to meet what would the end be. I cannot spend a week with you at Munich and at the end of the week bid you goodbye — saying "Goodbye, dear lady, I shall be passing here a year hence and will look forward to the pleasure of meeting you." This is the truth Gabrielle and this is why I do not go to Munich to meet you. But I shall always be glad to hear from you and to write to you and to send you my books.[2]

Very sincerely yours,

George Moore

[1] No doubt *Elizabeth Cooper*. Also see reference to it made in Letter 29.

[2] Several short excerpts of this letter are inaccurately transcribed in Hone, pp. 252-53.

Letter 28

Gabrielle to Moore   26 Juin [1904]

Dear Mr. Moore,

Your letter made me very happy. It was such a dear kind letter and I
thank you very much. We are friends again now and I so hope we never
shall quarrel again. I am glad my photo pleases you. Will you not send
me one of you? In my next letter I'll give you my new address. I cannot
write much to-day but I will from *chez mon amie.* I hope you will have
a nice summer. My dear great friend, I realy am very fond of you, and
it makes me so proud that you write such clever books. Good-bye now
and God bless you. Don't forget your

                            Gabrielle

And so you think we never, never will meet? Send me a photograph of
your portrait by Manet, will you? That is if you think it will please me.
No, I will give you the address at once but you must not forget it again!
Write to me: [address omitted in the typescript]. In your letter you say
such flattering things to me. I like it but it will make me quite conceited.

Letter 29

Moore to Gabrielle   12 July [1904]
                                                      4 Upper Ely Place
                                                      Dublin

My dear Gabrielle,

Your letter pleased me as much as your photograph, and now I really
know and really sympathise with my correspondent's kind sweet nature.
No wonder you wrote to me, instinct led you, and it led you aright — in
your subconscious nature you knew that you would find sympathy. I was
a little slow at guessing what you really are but now all doubts have
vanished, and for the future I will write to you as sincerely as you write
to me. I have just returned from London. Three weeks of dinner parties
operas and assemblies are enough and I am glad to get back to my writing. I have withdrawn myself snail like and I shall not leave my shell for
the next three months — in three months I shall have finished all my

works. I have rewritten *Evelyn Innes*.[1] I shall finish *The Lake* and a Comedy. The subject of my Comedy is a lady who writes to an author and in three acts I tell what happened to her and to him. If the Comedy is acted in Vienna you must go to see it. I think it will please you. I confess that your last letter has made me *really* anxious to see you — you are very charming and in the autumn I shall be free. As ever dear Gabrielle,[2]

George Moore

[1] First published in 1898 by T. Fisher Unwin, revised in 1901 and again in 1908. However, Moore is probably referring to preparations for the German translation (*Irdische und Himlische Lieb*) published in Berlin by Egon Fleischel in 1905.

[2] There is a brief excerpt of this letter in Hone, p. 253.

Letter 30

Moore to Gabrielle

1 August [1904]
4 Upper Ely Place
Dublin

My dear Gabrielle,

So now it is you who will not write. Well, it is ever thus. It was your last letters and your last photograph that won my heart and as I said in *Evelyn Innes* the moment a man falls in love the end is in sight, in a very short time he will lose the object of his love. I have lost mine before I ever saw her. Have you met someone who has distracted your attention from me or are you vexed because I said that I thought of writing a Comedy on the subject of an author's correspondence with a lady across the seas. Were I to meet you and tell you the frivolous little idea that came into my head you would be delighted with it — it is quite harmless and very complimentary to the lady. But if you do not wish the Comedy written I will not write it and you need not fear to write, "I would rather not" for I am surrounded by unfinished works and shall be glad, or very nearly glad, to get rid of one of them. Do write to me.

Always sincerely yours,

George Moore

Letter 31

Gabrielle to Moore   [October-November 1904]
                                  Böhmen, Austria

Dear Mr. Moore,
    I am here now at my brother's and won't return to Vienna before the beginning of December, so please don't go to Vienna now. My life is somewhat changed, you see, as I have to look after my brother's poor motherless little boy, and I *like* it as I am fond of babies. I'll send you some views of R. It is rather a beautiful place — a little gloomy perhaps, that is on rainy days. But I love it dearly. Dear Mr. Moore, write to me please. Tell me about your books. I think you have become quite lazy. Your last letter was in July (I think) and your last book[1] a year ago or more — I don't quite know. I think of you rather often. My new address in Vienna is: [address omitted], but you must write to here. Good-bye, my dear friend. I think you have forgotten all about your dear Gabrielle and Gabrielle doesn't like to be *traitée* like that! Last week it must have been a year that I first wrote to you.

                              G. v.H.

[1] Moore had sent her a copy of *The Untilled Field* in late November or early December 1903. See Letter 2.

Letter 32

Gabrielle to Moore   [Fall 1904?]

Dear Mr. Moore,
    You realy are not very nice to me and I know I shall *hate* your new book. Do you like Eva and Marietta better than me? Then of course you must not write to me again.

                              Gabrielle

Letter 33

Moore to Gabrielle

1 January 1906
4 Upper Ely Place
Dublin

My dear Gabrielle,

After this long time it will surprise you to hear from me, but you have heard that nothing is lost in this world. You have heard of the continuity of force. Why I never went to Vienna to see me [i.e., you] I cannot tell. I don't know myself but I feel I shall always regret not having gone for I am certain you are a charming woman, one whose charm I am capable of appreciating. I think what kept me from starting on this love adventure was the fear that you would be disappointed with me, and that we should just [be] angry with each other and with ourselves. Maybe I am wrong. Anyhow I know I shall always regret [it]. But what would life be without regret — regret is a mountain top on which which [sic] we stop and pout[?]. In view of the fact that I am sending you *The Lake* I should have said "there is a lake in every man's heart."[1] Sometimes one doesn't cross the lake. I wonder if you will be able to read the book; if you do read it I hope you will write to tell me what you think about it. I wonder if it is any good my telling you I am going to Bayreuth for certain this summer. I shall be there on the 25th of July; Bayreuth is not far from Vienna and you might like to see the performances; and at Bayreuth we should meet on neutral ground. I am going there with a young man, very rich, very young and very fascinating. Perhaps you will like him.[2] I think this is all I have to say at present. Goodbye, dear Gabrielle, I hope to hear from you and I am as ever,

Yours sincerely,

George Moore

[1] A quotation from the final paragraph of *The Lake*. In the 1905 Heinemann edition, Father Gogarty says, " 'There is a lake in every man's heart and every man must ungird his loins for the crossing.' " In the 1921 Heinemann edition, the line reads, " 'There is a lake in every man's heart and he listens to its monotonous whisper year by year, more and more attentive till at last he ungirds.' "

[2] Moore is probably referring to Thomas Evelyn Scott-Ellis, 8th Baron Howard de Walden and 4th Baron Seaford (1880-1946). Lord Howard de Walden was a writer, sportsman, and patron of the arts. He inherited great estates in London and elsewhere. He was editor and benefactor of *The Complete Peerage*, wrote several plays, and produced an operatic trilogy (as T. E. Ellis), with music by Joseph Holbrooke. He often accompanied Moore on trips to Bayreuth.

Letter 34

Moore to Gabrielle   17 February 1906
              4 Upper Ely Place
              Dublin

My dear Gabrielle,
It was a pleasure to me to receive your postcard and I have waited for you to redeem the promise therein to write me a letter. But no letter comes and it seems to me not unlikely that the delay is caused by the book I sent you. The story of *The Lake* is not one which would interest you; I am not sure that it interests me very much now. One gets in the hook of a subject just like a fish and the only way to get the hook out of one's gills is to write it. You will like my next book better. I am correcting the proofs of it now: *Memoirs of My Dead Life*,[1] that is its attractive title; I do not say my past life but my dead life — a little affectation intended to indicate that my love life is over. Think of it! If I had gone to Munich if I had made your acquaintance in that home of which you sent me a photograph, I might have written about you this year — you might be printing now. You will not take this seriously, the fancy just came up in my mind and I have jotted it down. I wonder if you will go to Bayreuth and if I shall meet you there. I am going there with a friend of mine, one of the richest men in England, a peer and a poet and a very considerable poet, young and good looking.[2] It would be a pity if we didn't meet after all this correspondence. Bayreuth is such a charming place to meet — I like the woods and the hills and the restaurants and the old cobblestones in the streets and the Margrave's Theatre.[3] Write to me at once and believe me to be

        Very sincerely yours,

        George Moore

[1] First published in June 1906 by Heinemann.

[2] Presumably Lord Howard de Walden.

[3] Named after the Margrave family of Bayreuth, renowned patrons of the arts in the eighteenth century. The Wagner festivals were held at the Festspielhaus, designed by the composer himself.

www.ingramcontent.com/pod-product-compliance
Lightning Source LLC
Chambersburg PA
CBHW060955120626
46557CB00003B/1173